Playing On Railroad Tracks

A Memoir

LEE ANN ROPES

SEO Strangers no more!

Lee Ann Ropes

10-20-19

Dedication

Dedicated to my family and friends, who have listened patiently as I rambled on about this book for many years. Thank you for your encouragement and for always believing in me.

And to you, Dad, the man I didn't know until I got to know myself.

Foreword

Maybe it's true that we all have a book lying dormant in us. I can't argue with that. I do know this story has been trying to work its way out of me for years, like a splinter festering on the bottom of one's foot.

I'll admit that patience is not one of my virtues. In recovery groups they call this a character defect, and it's one that is deeply rooted in my family. I've seldom heeded the advice that a watched pot never boils. My watched pot has been this manuscript.

A symptom of an addictive personality is to jump in head first at the beginning of any new project and expect to see the final result in the next breath. I've ignored the sage advice that life is a journey, not a destination. While others might still be in the planning stages, I have my key in the ignition and my eyes set on the finish line.

Do I often cross the finish line? No. Am I aware that I am missing the journey, the meat in the middle of the sandwich? I am, but I've never succeeded at slowing down.

So I gave birth to the concept of this book, believing I knew with certainty the beginning and the end of the story. It was all the pages in the middle that I couldn't seem to fill—the soul of my story. With great impatience, I found I couldn't put the pieces together. Was I telling the story of forgiveness between child and parent? Was I searching for something I'd left behind, or something I'd never found? Was I running away from or toward unnamable fears?

The answers didn't even begin to surface until long after I started writing. The loss of both parents prompted grief, anger,

1

and, ultimately, a searching look at myself. For survival, I knew instinctively that I had to write the story and uncover a way to let go of them and the past. I had no idea the answers would come as I began to deal with my own instability and mental issues. It seemed this imbalance permeated my family like a silent but deadly toxin. The diagnosis of bipolar disorder was the answer to my questions, the root of my pain, and, finally, the key to understanding.

Every one of the following written words moved me away from a shadowy place, real or imagined, that had held me in its darkness. The end of the story became the beginning of my story.

"This is the grace of the last years—the children coming to understand the contradictions in their parents, not to reconcile them but to encompass them in a larger love."

Janet Sternburg

Chapter One

Going Home

The slap came out of nowhere. The hand striking his face was a blow so forceful it sent his bifocal glasses flying, leaving a bloody, jagged gash across the bridge of his nose. There we sat in his brown pickup truck. He was seventy-two years old and dying. The hand that had just slapped him was mine—the hand of his own daughter.

I can still almost taste the day and the weather in vivid detail. We were country folks. Life to us was about Mother Nature. Most of our conversations were about the weather, the yard, how the farmers' crops were doing. This day was overcast with a sky a shade of gray that reminded me of field mice often seen darting in and out of small spaces in the fields. I musingly looked out at the cornfields that surrounded my parents' place and realized the cornstalks looked much like my high school's marching band members, evenly spaced and standing at attention. They reminded me I'd always wanted to be in the band, and that no amount of fast-talking could convince my dad that being in a silly band was worth the price of an instrument. I asked several times, but with the "no" came an accusation that being a part of the band was foolish and unimportant. I stopped asking.

It was September. The once plump cornstalks, now yellow and dry with maturity, waited for the combine that would harvest and transport them to their next destination. I knew their look well from a summer job during high school where I had toiled in the same fields, removing tassels from the corn. It was the hardest job I'd ever had. I never figured out which was worse—being transported like livestock to the fields on flatbed trucks, the pitiful pay, or having to sneak off to a deserted corn row each time you needed to heed Mother Nature's call. Most of the young detasslers, as we were called, didn't last until the end of the summer. It was grueling and I was one of those that gave up.

Today the wind was whistling and blowing dried brush around in the yard. I looked up and noticed that the leaves on all of Dad's cherished maple trees were twisted inside out as they often are when nature knows rain is coming long before the local weatherman does. I knew the rain was coming, but I hadn't forseen the storm that was about to hit.

I'd only been back in Indiana a month and suddenly I'd been confronted with the reason I'd fled so many years ago. That cause had been sitting next to me in the truck a few minutes before. Dressed in his usual plaid, short-sleeved flannel shirt and dark work pants, he was balding, thin, and weathered from many years of work in a blue-collar world. His razor-sharp tongue was honed, as usual, and his piercing words, which had left me emotionally bleeding many times as a child, had just spun us into the only physical confrontation we had ever had. We argued. I couldn't understand why he didn't understand my intentions for coming home. It seemed so obvious to me. He and Mom were sick. They needed me. I was there to help.

I followed him to the truck and got in as I tried to explain that his negative attitude wasn't contributing anything positive to his health or to the situation at hand. The angry words flew back and forth between us.

"No one asked you to come here. I don't need or want your help. And I don't like your attitude. I never have," he spewed at me as his face turned a deeper shade of red with each word.

My world came to a halt with those stinging words, and that's when I reached out and slapped him. Then I pushed the passenger door open and ran from the truck. It was the same feeling I'd had as a child running away from one of his spankings with a belt. I never looked back, but I could hear him burning rubber all the way down the driveway.

Home. Sweet. Home.

Chapter Two

It isn't difficult to describe Florida weather in the summer. Hot. Hot. Hot. It is particularly uncomfortable when you are trying to dress for work as I was this morning. I hadn't been out of the shower fifteen minutes and I was already breaking into a sweat.

Heading out the door, I heard my cell phone ringing. As usual, I started the frantic search through my purse to locate it. One ring, then two, then three. I reminded myself of my love/hate relationship with oversized purses—plenty of room to carry everything and plenty of room to lose everything. I referred to the location of any item going into one of these voluminous bags as being in the bottom of the birdcage. Finally, on the fourth ring and with the aid of a few curse words, I managed to fish the phone off the bottom.

"Hello."

"Sis, I have some bad news," my sister said.

There were no words of greeting or small talk like there usually was between Julie and me. We didn't talk often. She settled back in Indiana and I had been in Florida for many years, so we just checked in with each other occasionally. We were never close as children, and adulthood had not changed that. Our conversations usually centered around our parents.

I barely recognized her voice. It was thin and scratchy like one of the cheap bath towels Mom loved to get free in boxes of laundry soap. Between her sobs I was able to discern just a couple words—*Dad* and *cancer*.

I tried to respond, but couldn't catch my breath. It felt like the pointed tip of a boot kicked me right in the gut. I finally said, "Oh, my God. I'm not where I can talk right now. Let me call you back, Julie." I stared out the window with the phone still in my hand.

Out my car window I could see that even the pavement was steaming. The air was humid and sticky like cotton candy. I couldn't believe that earlier that morning I was thinking it might be a good day to just skip lunch and leave the office for a double-dipped cone of chocolate or vanilla ice cream. My sister's call had changed all that. In addition to my mom's cancer, which had been diagnosed months earlier, Dad had cancer, too. In a split second, my world changed from a double-dipped cone to a double-dose of cancer. Both parents sick at the same time? Unbelievable.

Six months earlier, Mom's diagnosis was colon cancer. As if that news wasn't bad enough, during her surgery she experienced a rare and near-deadly reaction to the anesthesia Placed in a medically induced coma for three weeks, her chances of survival changed daily, like Indiana weather in the springtime.

Dad, Julie and I spent what felt like three years locked up in the hospital waiting room. It became our makeshift home. Julie and I fidgeted and paced like caged animals at the zoo. We played cards to pass the time. Relatives arrived, talked, and left, and then more relatives arrived, talked, and left. We watched the clock on the wall like Cinderella worrying about midnight. However, unlike Cinderella, hers was a fairy tale and ours was a nightmare. Her curfew was midnight, but we had no curfew or timeline for the end our adventure.

The face on the clock became our enemy, and the room itself wasn't very friendly, either, and became more unsightly with each passing day. If you weren't depressed when you arrived, the dreary décor would put you under. Filled with gray, upholstered furniture along gray, scratched-up walls, even the glow from the fluorescent lights looked gray. After several days, I noticed adding to the ambience of the room were the dingy lights flickering with each announcement that came over the public address system. A small vase of silk flowers pathetically loitered in the corner, ugly and alone like the junior high girl no one chooses for a dance. The vase was cracked and the purple flowers drooped from the weight of dusty leaves.

On the third day of Mom's hospitalization as I was flipping through the television channels for the hundredth time, we heard voices nearing the doorway. Around the corner came another posse of relatives. This time it was my aunt on my mother's side, her live-in boyfriend Bob, and other assorted first and second cousins. From a distance, the encounter must have sounded and looked like a party, but surely the sterile surroundings and shiny linoleum floors would quickly clarify that misconception.

"Well, look who's here," said my cousin Vicki. "We couldn't find you guys. We wandered all over this darned place."

Vicki was a third cousin, one that had been married and divorced so many times most of us had lost track. The last tidbit I'd heard about her was that her current boyfriend had gone to prison for charge card fraud. I thought it best not to bring up the topic.

I turned around just in time to hear my aunt yell, "Annie! Look at you. It's been so long since we've seen you. When did you get in?"

"I've been in town since Thursday," I said.

I tried not to stare at my aunt's teeth. There weren't many of them, and the ones that had survived looked like they were on life support. Her skin was rough like a wooden deck that had never been weather treated—cracked from sun exposure and bloated from moisture absorption. Her hair looked brittle and wiry just like Mom's hair had gotten from the harsh chemicals and damage left behind from years of home permanent treatments. Adding to the mess was the fact that her hair looked like it hadn't met up with a brush in years. None of this seemed to bother her as she asked, "How's Martha today? Have the doctors explained what's going on with her?"

"Yes and no. The prognosis seems to change from hour to hour," I replied. "Each time we see a doctor, they seem to have a different concern from the last time they talked to us." I was trying to keep my answers short and succinct because I dreaded the idea of having to explain all the medical details over and over again, especially when they were so vague and negative.

We spent the next few hours talking about our lives since the last time we'd seen each other. My sister hadn't seen them in years, either, even though she lived only twenty or thirty miles away from them. In spite of my contemptuous and judgmental attitude, I couldn't help but be entertained by their animation and tendency to be rough around the edges. Their voices were loud and raucous. They laughed frequently and with unbridled energy. There was no pretentiousness, and yet they irritated me.

One cousin turned toward me and asked, "Girl, are you still married to that rich guy? Your mom told us all about him. He has his own airplane?" she asked.

"Nope. Mom's not keeping you very well informed. I got rid of him years ago."

"What! Are you crazy, girl? With all that money?" she asked incredulously.

I wondered if Mom had exaggerated her stories, although I suspected even the bare bones truth about my ex-husband's status probably blew them away. Compared to their lives, chances were that mine sounded like a dream.

John, ex-husband number two, was a self-made millionaire at an early age. He was the most intelligent man I'd ever met, and was living a champagne lifestyle compared to my six-pack of beer existence when I first met him. He had told me he was intrigued by my Midwestern values and naiveté, and I was profoundly impressed by his sense of adventure and financial means to fulfill his dreams. We traveled the world, drank the finest of wines, and, most importantly, brought two beautiful daughters into the world. My cousin's comments reminded me that I had often questioned my decision to abandon the relationship and the life he had provided. The thought was still painful even after so many years.

The cousins continued their interrogation with the gusto and energy one sees from the contestants on television game shows. Each of my answers gave way to another question. It was the getting to know each other routine. I pretended to be interested in their lives, which, in my opinion, probably consisted of the morbid and mundane— grandchildren out of wedlock, AIDS, and unemployment were the headliners. I kept thinking to myself that I could never live the way they did. Though I barely knew them, I saw snapshots of hopelessness and discontent in their lives. I found myself pondering the impossibility that we came from the same genetic line. They were so different than the image I had of myself. I had no doubt their existence was a gloomy one, filled with nothingness and narrow-mindedness. They amused and appalled me. It never occurred to me that my opinion of them was clouded by my own narrow-mindedness.

Our voices lowered to hushed tones as the conversation returned to talk of Mom's condition and her chances. At times the room fell silent and I squirmed with discomfort. Several times when this happened, I saw my sister reach over to touch one of the relatives' hands or legs in a gesture of support. Julie seemed to be comforted by these people. I found this hard to understand because I sure wasn't. She was our mom and I felt some resentment with their presence. Their tackiness was beginning to wear on my nerves. They were quickly becoming the embodiment of the many caustic remarks Dad spewed over the years when referring to Mom's side of the family.

Mom didn't see or mention her family often, but when she did, Dad always added some nasty comments.

"Oh, that's a fine group of relatives you have there. Do any of them have jobs? How many are in jail now? Trailer trash. That's what we call 'em.'"

Mom's only response was usually something demure like, "Oh, Garold. They're not all that bad."

As I listened to these conversations, I began to realize that you can talk honestly and negatively about your own family, but when someone else makes those observations, it cuts like a knife. I guess Dad didn't understand that concept, or just didn't care. He must have been blind to the humiliation I saw in Mom's eyes.

Just as I was excusing myself from the hospital waiting room, Dad arrived. Each time he showed up at the hospital, I felt a knot in my stomach. His social skills were unpredictable and I feared the worst. If he liked you, he liked you. If he didn't care for you, a ninety-degree room could turn to ice in seconds.

I gave Dad a quick update on the few changes with Mom, and then I excused myself. There were too many people in the room. I'd seen enough explosions in my life. I wasn't hanging around for the one that might happen next.

Chapter Three

Early on the following rainy Monday morning, Mom took a turn for the worse. We paced the hospital hallways. Every nurse's station looked the same, and the aroma from the cafeteria smelled like disinfectant instead of food.

Trying to decide whether to go home or stay, I found myself standing at the doorway of a small chapel. I hesitated, but gingerly took a few steps inside. The small rays of light from the stained-glass windows washed the tiny room in a soft, pink glow. Two candles burned at a wooden altar where several flowers had been randomly placed by other worried souls, I guessed. I bent down on my knees. I acknowledged for the first time that Mom's condition was out of our control.

My prayer was short. "Whoever you are, and if you are listening, please watch over my mom and help us to accept the outcome." I remained kneeling for a few minutes waiting for the possibility of an answer. None came. And although I wasn't sure why, I felt a sense of strength and peace as I left the room.

It wasn't my first prayer during this ordeal. Dad had asked my sister and me to pray almost every night since Mom had gotten sick. I was puzzled by his request because I had never seen him express any kind of belief in faith before. A discussion of his mother's devout religious doctrines were about as close as we ever came to the subject.

Dad called Grandma's church congregation the Holy Rollers, and often questioned the intentions and morality of their much adored

Pastor Jim. All through childhood we listened to his concerns about how much money Grandma was donating to the "damn church." We also heard he and Mom talking about the members of the church speaking in tongues.

Grandma's church was her life. Mom once told us that Grandma Nellie didn't even come to her and Dad's wedding because it was on her church night. I remember thinking that was pretty harsh. And even though most of the time she couldn't even hear what was being said due to hearing loss, she was devoted and nearly giddy when she talked about going to church. Grandma would occasionally invite us all to join her at church, and although disappointed, I'm sure, she never seemed really surprised when Dad declined.

One year for Grandma's birthday, my aunt coerced all her brothers to surprise their mother and attend service. It was the first time I'd ever seen my father in a suit. My sister and I thought he looked like a mannequin, but he didn't laugh when we told him that. Instead, he tugged at his tie swearing he would never do this again. We knew better than to pursue the subject. We waited until he went outside before we started to laugh again.

Once we arrived at church there was no containing our amusement. All four of Dad's brothers in suits looked like mannequins, too. The more Mom shushed us, the harder my sister and I laughed. It wasn't until Dad shot us one of his looks that we stopped. From that point on, I didn't dare look over at my sister, because even the fear of Dad's wrath would not have prevented me from starting to laugh again.

The church was mammoth, mysterious, and beautiful. I felt so small because it was so big. And it was dark. The seats were dark wood and so were the walls. Everything was dark except the gleaming stained-glass windows. I was fascinated by their sheer size and brilliant colors. They reminded me of the kaleidoscopes we had once played with.

13

The service seemed to go on for hours and was boring. I noticed the adults around us were squirming almost as much as we were. My sister and I had been forced to wear dresses, along with Mom's admonishment to act like ladies. Julie entertained herself by pulling on a loose thread she'd found at the bottom of her dress. I could picture her unraveling the entire frock and exiting the church in her birthday suit. Mom gave Dad the elbow several times when she noticed his eyes closed. My sister and I managed to stay awake because we were waiting for the tongue thing to happen. We didn't want to miss that, whatever it was.

Julie and I were whispering to Mom asking for gum when suddenly the organ music started. It was really loud and seemed to be coming from every direction. The congregation began to sing with the kind of passion I'd only seen from Dad during basketball games on television. The folks also kept reaching upward with their hands as they sang the hymns, swaying their bodies back and forth with their eyes closed. We weren't sure what all that was about, but my sister and I decided to try it anyway, until Mom gave us the elbow, too.

Dad was evidently confused just like us. As the congregants sang, they began to leave their pews and travel up and down the aisles, hands still in the air, and tears in their eyes. Everyone seated near us heard Dad's sigh of relief as he stood, reached in his pocket, and pulled out his car keys. He had mistakenly thought everyone was headed toward the exit, and he was not a happy man when Mom pulled him down into the seat and explained otherwise. No one was leaving. They were up and moving because they were happy and filled with the spirit of the Holy Ghost.

Julie and I spent the rest of the service with our heads lowered and shoulders bobbing up and down as we tried to hide our faces and restrain our laughter without looking Dad's way. We decided on the way home that Dad had inadvertently made church pretty fun, even though we were disappointed that we never spotted any unusual tongue activity.

The memory of that long ago service was the first and last time I had seen Dad in church, so I was surprised he was asking us to pray while Mom was in the hospital. Maybe Mom's critical condition had scared the cynic right out of him, just like Grandma told us kids that Jesus could scare the devil out of you. Dad continued to remind us each evening, "Girls, don't forget to pray for Mom."

One night after we'd said good night, it occurred to me that this one small request from him had given me a sliver of credence toward religion. I remembered a time of crisis during my first marriage when I discovered my new husband was smoking marijuana every weekend. Naive, and hysterical with emotion, I placed a call to my parents crying that my husband was a drug addict. After a moment of silence, my dad calmly encouraged me to go to the small church we had been attending and talk to the minister.

At the time I minimized his spiritual response, but now many years later, I saw its relevance in a new light. After all, if Dad believed in the validity of religion, then maybe it was true. Hadn't we always blindly followed his lead? It felt almost like we were on the same team, even if it was a praying team. It had a family feel to it. That hadn't happened often. It felt good. It actually felt right.

I was also surprised to get a peek at Dad's superstitious nature. I had never seen this part of his personality, either. He asked that we avoid a certain country road as we drove each day to the hospital. Apparently, two days in a row, a black cat crossed his path there.

I knew the road well. When we were young, a mother rabbit had lost her life to Dad's lawn mower. We set about raising her three babies despite the skeptics who told us we would never be successful. Three months and hundreds of eyedropper feedings later, our baby rabbits had grown to young adults. With tearful eyes, we released them into the wild on the very road that had now obviously spooked Dad.

Julie and I were paralyzed with fear at the thought of losing Mom, so we followed Dad's every instruction and steered clear of the bad road.

We also saw Dad's domestic side emerge while Mom was sick.

"I just called Dad. You won't believe what he told me," my sister said. "He is doing a load of laundry and baking bread! And he sounds very proud of himself, too!"

He was cooking. He was cleaning. He was turning into freaking Susie Homemaker. We teased him incessantly about his new homemaking abilities. Up to this point, the limit of his domestic skills was making a mean bologna and cheese sandwich, and sometimes he even required assistance for that task.

During one of our many trips to the hospital, my sister asked, "Annie, have you noticed how mellow Dad has been since Mom's been in the hospital? I hesitate to say it for fear I'll ruin it, but he's been much nicer. What's up with that?"

"Beats me," I replied. "It's as if fear has melted his tough exterior a little. I've heard very few nasty comments from him since I got here. Maybe he's getting soft in his old age."

"I wish," said my sister with a sigh.

Three weeks later on a sunny, Thursday morning while Dad and I were having coffee, he spotted a robin in the backyard.

"Look! There's a robin," he said, pointing out toward one of his pine trees. "That's the first one I've seen this year. They're back. That's a good sign," Dad said, smiling ear to ear.

"Oh, I see it, Dad! Look, there's another one!" I said, pointing toward the barn.

He and Mom adored robins. Each year their arrival was joyfully met as a sign that warm weather was approaching, and likewise their departure brought sad resignation that winter was hiding out right around the corner.

"I'll have to tell your mom this morning that the robins are back. Their showing up will make her happy," said Dad as he got up to leave for the hospital.

I watched him as he pulled out of the driveway. He sure seemed different. Was it possible he had mellowed, or was he so scared of losing Mom that we were experiencing only a respite from his harsh ways? I hoped for the former and feared the later.

Our prayers, the right pavement, and, of course, the robins must have worked a miracle. On her twenty-first day of captivity, the doctors told us that Mom was in the clear. She would need chemotherapy but would recover. Later the same day, we had no doubts she was on the mend when she got busted smoking a cigarette in her hospital room. Dad laughed when the hospital called to tell us of Mom's indiscretion. He said, "We better bring the ol' gal home before she gets kicked out of that place!"

Now, less than six months later, it appeared Mom had recovered, although we sometimes questioned her mental capacity in certain areas. There was just something different about her—an aloofness and a disconnect that wasn't there before the surgery. Dad, on the other hand, had used Mom's recovery months to slowly return to his former grumpy, moody self, although he was a little less sarcastic than before.

Life was just about back to routine, but my sister's news had abruptly ended that. Dad was now part of the exclusive cancer club as well. My mind raced like it did after my third cup of coffee. I gasped with desperation at the thought that surely there was some obscure law of statistics prohibiting both of your parents from having this disease simultaneously. Damn the statistics. If they existed, they had failed us miserably.

Following my sister's phone call, I couldn't make myself get out of the car and go into the office. I had to force myself to call her back.

"My God, Julie. What are we going to do?" I asked as I felt my eyes filling with tears.

"I don't know, sis." There was a long pause of silence before she said, "I don't have a damn clue."

Chapter Four

George Orwell once described how childhood necessarily creates a false map of the world we live in. But since it is the only map we have, no matter how old we are when trouble strikes, we take off running to those fabulous (and fictitious) places our minds have created. I couldn't see any choice but to pack up and go to Indiana. Both of my parents were sick and I had to be there. There was no doubt in my mind that it was what I needed to do—well, almost no doubt.

For anyone who ever thought of running away from home as a child, my passion and illogical reasoning was similar. In reality, I put as much thought into the decision as the runaway child who takes off on his journey with no destination in mind and with just a pair of underwear and a stuffed animal. In the second it took me to make what would become a life-altering decision, I spontaneously tossed to the wind thoughts of my children, my job, and my life. Consequences never once penetrated my state of temporary insanity.

I had a dead end job in a real estate office. My latest divorce had left me with a broken family, and my instinct was to run toward the fire like a moth drawn to a light. The fire was my family of origin. Although separated from them for years, the power of an invisible tether between us pulled at me.

I knew there was little doubt that the frustrating phone calls with my parents over the last six months had helped to fuel my insanity. Unlike my generation that was prone to challenge any diagnosis or decision of anyone or anything, my parents' generation still looked on the medical profession as untouchable and hero-like in their authority. From their perspective, to challenge a doctor would be to disrespect them. I could barely even prod them to ask the doctor questions. They were arriving home after doctor appointments with bags full of medications and heads full of confusion regarding diagnosis, prognosis, and follow-up.

"The doctor told us I may need surgery," Mom explained during her illness.

"When will he know for sure?" I asked.

"Um, I don't know."

"Does he have to run more tests?" There was silence on the other end. "Is he going to call you to let you know?" I asked, trying to keep my frustration at bay.

"I'm not sure, honey. He said so much I just can't remember." She yelled, "Garold, do you remember if the doctor was going to call us, or what?"

"Hell, I don't know, Martha," Dad yelled back. "You were there, too. Damn doctors get paid the big bucks. You'd think they could at least speak English so you could understand what the hell they're saying."

I muttered under my breath, "Oh, my God, this is so ridiculous."

I tried persuading them to take a tape recorder so they could play back his words when they got home, but no. Mustn't embarrass ourselves in front of the omnipotent physician.

"Do you at least know what the new medicine is for?" Silence again. "Mom, did you ask him *any* questions?"

I could picture her on the other end shaking her head no and shrugging her shoulders like a little girl being scolded. I knew I was guilty of that scolding more than once. There were many times when I just couldn't hide my irritation.

"Does the end justify the means?" I asked myself, knowing well I knew the answer. My anger was misdirected, but I couldn't stop myself from making them my target. Many times after conversations with them, I realized with disgust, that I had sounded just like Dad. I didn't want to hurt them, but as hard as I tried on the next phone call, the result was often the same. The dialogue after each doctor appointment was maddening. Rationality aside, I told myself I should be there to accompany them to their doctor appointments. I could ask questions. I could take charge. It was all about me. Not once was it what do *they* need or want.

Chapter Five

Just like cancer and many other catastrophic illnesses, alcoholism is considered a family disease. No one escapes the pain and scars from the drama of a family member in the throes of this kind of monster. I had firsthand experience with this from my own childhood—from my own parents. What I didn't recognize was the impact the scars had on every decision I had made in the past and was about to make for the future.

In the office where I worked, gossip traveled almost as fast as the donuts leaving the kitchen in the morning. By the end of the first day of my decision to go back to Indiana, nearly all my fellow coworkers had already heard the news and many had an opinion about it.

"You're moving again?" asked a friend and colleague. "Do you know how many different phone numbers I've had for you over the years?"

I thought I noticed a touch of disbelief, and maybe even a little sarcasm, in her voice.

"Yep," I replied. "I know. I've lost track, too." I laughed as I walked away.

The truth was, she was right. I'd moved so many times and changed jobs so frequently, I'd long ago given up on a real career. Forty different jobs in forty different fields had me feeling like tumbleweed blowing aimlessly across a lonely, barren prairie. When responding to help wanted ads, my first task was to make sure I hadn't worked there before.

Leaving a job wasn't usually about the pay or the job itself. The decision to leave was always about not fitting in, and a restlessness that said to move on. Restlessness and discontent—two conditions I would eventually learn were hallmarks of the addictive personality and certain personality disorders. From radio disc jockey to dog trainer to singing telegram messenger, no one could accuse me of a dull life. Like my phone numbers and addresses, one had better use a pencil with an eraser instead of a pen to note the name of my latest employer.

I tried explaining to those interested, and probably those who weren't, that I wasn't without doubts about going back home to help my parents. Most of them asked why. My boss mentioned that my responsibility was to my daughters. But my emotions kept bubbling to the surface, drowning out any voices of reason, including his. They just didn't understand. They couldn't comprehend the sense of responsibility I felt, a sense I never would have recognized while I was still drinking alcohol. But now I was sober. I believed my thinking was clear and rational. Later, I would hear the idea that when you sober up a horse thief, you have a horse thief who's not drinking. In my case, it turned out to be a sober person who still had a brain that wasn't working properly.

My second recovery from alcohol abuse started after thirteen years of abstinence. I was recently divorced, met a drinking man, and picked up a drink. As they say in rooms of recovery, I was off to the races. Eighteen months later and still drinking, I was wallowing in a state of emotional bankruptcy and mental instability. I gave notice at work, mortgaged my home, and checked myself into an alcohol and drug treatment center for twenty-eight days in Antigua.

Now, having just celebrated my first year of sobriety, I convinced myself I was healthy enough to make good decisions. My parents were elderly and sick. I believed I could rescue them. I felt like I understood myself and my recovery this time, even though my newfound life was still tenuous and rocky. I tried to look at the pros and cons of the situation. There were many cons, including no money, my two daughters living with their dad, and myself still uncomfortable in my own skin, one of the many reasons I drank to begin with.

In Indiana, I would be over a thousand miles away from my girls and immersed in a world of drinkers. Sick or not, I was pretty sure my parents hadn't given up their daily cocktails, and I sure didn't want to give up my sobriety. I had heard many recovering drunks say, "Hang out in a barbershop long enough and you'll get a haircut."

I didn't need or want *that* salon service. A shudder of fear passed through me as I thought about it, but I was quickly sidelined as another coworker stopped by my cubicle to verify the rumor that I was moving. As I told her the details, I heard myself describing old behavior, the kind we try to leave behind once we are in recovery. One of the mantras in twelve step programs is not to make any big changes the first year of recovery. Quitting my job. Leaving my friends and family behind. Moving to another state. No big changes, huh?

For the first time, I was putting together all the dangerous pieces of the puzzle I was about to create when my phone rang. It was my sister. Dad was having problems breathing. They had him in the emergency room. I wanted to know all the details, but mostly I wanted to be there with them.

Once again, the realization of the big changes I was about to make was instantly buried beneath fear, frustration, and the uncon-scious compulsion to be on the front line and in charge of the battle. I was to discover that this urge to be the star of the show was another characteristic of alcoholism. We tend to want to be the stage director, or not involved at all.

Chapter Six

Tuesday morning dawned and that meant the weekly office meeting that was mandatory for all support staff and realtors. The sound of the alarm clock pierced my slumber and abruptly ended a terrible dream I was having. I knew the minute my eyes opened that it was one of those nightmares that would take half the day to shake off. I'd always had them, but they were coming more often since Dad's diagnosis. In this one, someone was chasing me and I kept trying to dial 911, but I had no reception on my cell phone. Damn cell phones, I thought. They aren't even reliable in your dreams.

This dream had taken me back many years to my junior high school days and to one of the many nights when Dad came home liquored up. That evening the battle was louder than usual. I woke up to the sound of a scream. I snuck out of my bedroom and crept quietly down the hallway. In the kitchen, I saw my mother sitting in a chair that was tipped backward, struggling to fight off my drunken father who had his hands around her throat.

"Dad! Dad! Stop it! Dad!" I yelled as I ran toward them. When my screams didn't break his chokehold, I hit and pulled him until he finally let go of her. He turned and looked at me with a blank stare. As his rage quickly subsided, his look turned into one of bewilderment, and his demeanor took on the appearance of a puppy after being caught urinating on the carpet. I was not impressed with that look. We'd had lots of puppies in our family. I knew a puppy's behavior could be forgiven because of age and a lack of training. I was pretty damn sure Dad didn't fit into either of those categories. Forgiveness didn't apply here.

With just enough time to catch our breaths and make an attempt to recover from the scene we had witnessed, the drunk passed out in a chair and began to snore, leaving us to clean up the emotional mess he had just dumped on us. I got ice for Mom's throat, and my sister and I, the little ones who needed to be comforted, tried to comfort her. As she wiped at her tears, Mom's voice was small and trembling. "That son of a bitch. It's the damn liquor. It makes him crazy."

Confused, and with a mix of sadness and anger, I put my hand into hers and whispered, "If that's true, Mom, why do they sell liquor?"

She pulled me toward her and held me tight, but didn't answer. I would be well into adulthood before I was introduced to the concept of codependency. Then I would look back and understand that denial can be bliss and very intoxicating.

So grateful the dream had ended, I hurriedly slipped into my favorite jeans and a shirt and headed off to work. As I did many mornings, I called Mom as I left the house. Since the day I'd left home after high school, we had talked on the phone at least once every day. We didn't discuss much other than the weather and the grandchildren, but we touched base daily, nonetheless.

The truth was, I had learned years before never to call my parents anytime after six o'clock in the evening. It was, after all, the bewitching hour when chances were pretty good any contact would find them half in the bag with alcohol. There was nothing I needed to say worth the disappointment of hearing their slurred voices. I'd heard enough of that over the years.

I was in fifth grade when I first noticed the effects alcohol had on Mom. I was used to Dad's drinking, but the first few times I came home from school and found Mom tipsy, it took me by surprise.

Usually she was in a good mood and apologized for having had a few beers while she cleaned the house, which she readily and frequently declared was her least favorite task. But by seventh grade, the house cleaning sessions became more frequent, the apologies stopped, and more often than not when she and Dad went out for the evening, she came home in no better shape than he did. I learned to live with the possibility that bringing a friend home from school could become an embarrassing situation. One never knew how 'clean' the house would be or how many liquid refreshments Mom might have consumed.

During the first year of my airline career, I invited Mom to fly to Ft. Myers, Florida, and meet me for Mother's Day. I was scheduled for a twenty-hour layover in a beautiful hotel and looked forward to spending the time with her. Mom's flight arrived a little earlier than mine. Once all my passengers deplaned, I hurried down the jetway eager to find her. The minute I saw her, she stood up, and panic washed over me. Her appearance was disheveled and she staggered as she walked toward me. Following directly behind me was my crew—captain, co-captain, and all the flight attendants. In front of me was my drunken mother.

"Annie! Hi, honey," she bellowed in a voice that surely could have been heard in the next concourse. As she approached with outstretched arms, I could feel the heat of embarrassment rush through my body and a flash of dread engulf me.

"It's so good to see you, hon. I had a great flight. The flight attendants were very generous with those little bottles. I'm afraid I had too many," she said as she leaned over, thinking she was whispering near my ear.

I was finding it hard to catch my breath while trying to act like nothing was wrong. I wanted to run and pretend like I didn't know her, but before I could, she laced her arm through mine and leaned heavily into me as she asked no more than two inches from my face

27

in a voice that had grown louder and grating again, "Aren't you going to introduce me to everyone?"

Little did I know the worst was yet to come. Being short and stocky never made it easy for anyone to get into a van like the one waiting to pick us up outside the airport. But being short, stocky, and snockered made the maneuver impossible. After making several futile attempts to get her foot on the running board, I watched in horror as the captain and two male flight attendants literally hoisted my mother into her seat inside the van.

Once we reached the hotel, the guys got her out of the van, and I managed to get her to the room right before she passed out. I spent the rest of the evening sitting in a chair in the corner, watching the television with no sound as Mom snored away our Mother's Day celebration.

The next morning when she awoke wearing the same clothes as the night before, she wore a pained expression that I recognized from my drinking days and from literature I'd read in recovery. It wasn't just a hangover. It was a look of pitiful and incomprehensible demoralization. As hard as I tried, I couldn't help feeling a little sorry for her. I tried reminding myself that she wasn't used to flying and getting away was a big deal for her. I'd had those same feelings when I first started flying.

It took some time that morning for us to make eye contact. When we did, her apology failed to make a dent in my disappointment and disgust. I was too hurt to forgive. The air between us was icy and awkward, just the way I remembered it being between my parents as I was growing up. We barely said good-bye as she boarded her plane for home. She was gone in an instant, but the shame endured for years. For both of us.

It was the last time we ever made arrangements to meet on one of my layovers.

Chapter Seven

My mother was born Martha June Mitchell, and she was a real character. The youngest of six children born to very poor parents, she didn't talk much about her childhood, but when she did, there was an undeniable sadness just below the surface of her words. Then just as quickly as she was sad, she was happy again.

She was adamant in her aversion to antiques, or old junk as she called them. Anytime I admired an old collectible in a store, she would turn away saying, "That's ugly. It looks and smells like the stuff we had when I was a kid."

Mom was pretty sedentary. We teased her that she moved from the refrigerator to the kitchen table to the garage to the car and back, and that was about it. She wore cloth slippers from Walmart and dared anyone to make fun of them. She shuffled along rather than actually picking up her feet to walk. That is, unless the bell on the dryer went off. Then you'd find her yelling for help and moving like a sprinter in the direction of the sound. Everyone in the family knew that if you were in hearing distance of that bell, you'd better hustle over to where she would be frantically pulling clothes out of the dryer and hanging them up quickly so they didn't wrinkle. She hated ironing like a surfer hates flat seas. In the years before she learned that dryer technique, she often offered to pay me to iron. I was promised five cents per piece unless it had to be sprinkled or wet ironed, and then I got ten cents a piece. I thought it was good deal, although I don't remember her ever actually paying me.

Martha June, or Mugs as her siblings called her, grew up with three sisters and two brothers. She once told us that she had overheard her mom telling someone that she, as the youngest, had been a mistake. Her recollection brought about a look of pain on her face that only a parent you love can inflict.

Martha June was adamant about her hatred for housework. She did, however, go to great trouble every spring to empty out all the closets and hang all the clothes outside on the clothesline. My sister and I marveled that she went to such lengths just so the clothes smelled like fresh air. We found out when we got older that her mom had performed the very same spring ritual.

Her daily routine was pretty simple and predictable. Along with robins, she loved diet soda, soap operas, and the *Price is Right* show, along with its host Bob Barker. She very seldom missed a show. She seemed quite content to sit out in the garage at her card table that was always covered in some flowered, plastic tablecloth. Near her soda would be her cigs, television remote, and the portable phone. My sister and I, and even Dad, called it "Mom's office."

We figured like all parents, she had her quirks. Dad liked to talk about the one where Mom listened in on other people's phone calls.

"You kids don't remember, you were much too young, but we used to have party telephone lines. Lots of folks in the same neighborhood used the same phone lines. Well, your mother loved to listen in. I'd catch her doing it all the time," Dad explained.

"Oh, not all the time," Mom said, trying to defend herself without giggling. "But there was this one, nasty, fat woman I couldn't stand and I'll admit I did overhear a couple of her conversations!"

Dad looked over at us and winked. "See? I told you so! The old heifer is nosey!" he said. "And she listened to more than a few of that woman's phone calls!"

Mom's quirks kept us entertained. Much to our chagrin, she kept her dentures in the bathroom, right out in the open where everyone could see them in a little yellow cup with a lamb decal on it. The cup was a relic from my sister's childhood. The more we complained about her chops, as she called them, the more she laughed and reveled in our disgust. As she got older, she started misplacing her teeth. Several times she called one of us saying, "You're not going to believe this. I did it again. I can't for the life of me figure out where I put my teeth." We came to a new appreciation for the little cup with the lamb on it and the grief it had saved us from.

Perhaps like many mothers and daughters, Mom was always good at reading me, even over the phone. As hard as I might try to hide it when something was amiss, she could always tell by the sound of my voice.

On the surface, and unlike Dad, Mom wasn't a complicated person. She certainly wasn't high maintenance. She didn't take life too seriously unless you messed with her cigarettes or her afternoon naps. Those were sacred. A description of her would probably be missing the words diva or epicurean of life. A more befitting characterization would read, "A woman with no personal rights."

She lived in Dad's shadow. She went where he decided to go, and she ate and slept when he decided she would. She got to go out when it was his choice. Many times I watched her watch him. Sometimes her gaze had a touch of respect in it, and at other times it was tinged with a look of apprehension, perhaps anticipating his next tantrum or harsh word. When he did or said something that really ticked her off, she would wait until he was out of the room and then thumb her nose at him. Her gesture caused my sister and me to double over with laughter. But I also asked myself why she didn't stand up to him. Why couldn't she, or didn't she, speak her mind and defend herself?

Mom was a character unlike any other mother we knew. We couldn't depend on her to be a warrior defending herself or to pay us for chores, but we could always count on her for a good laugh. She was always quick to laugh at herself, and my sister and I learned at a young age that it was fun and acceptable to laugh along with her. She was extremely proud of her parallel parking skills, but we found out one afternoon that those skills, although quite good, had certain boundaries. I recall an afternoon where her antics had my sister and me laughing unncontrollably.

Having circled the downtown area several times searching for a parking space, we all shouted at once when we spotted an available spot just ahead on the right. Mom whipped the car into position and started her parallel parking moves. Unfortunately, there was an elderly man standing on the sidewalk next to our spot and he decided to give this female driver a helping hand in parking. Mom spotted him waving his hands to motion her in. She swore. She pulled forward and then prepared to back in again. This time the old man stepped off the sidewalk and into the parking space to give her even more animated hand signals. Her entire body tensed up and her voice got shrill as she let more cuss words fly. She pulled forward and tried one more time to back in with the old man now using not only his hands, but also yelling instructions this time. I wondered if the man had any idea he was risking his life standing in that parking spot. With one final jerk of the car, so violent it caused my sister and me to lunge forward in our seats, Mom hit the gas and ran the back wheel of the car right up onto the sidewalk. I was afraid to look back to see the man's face. She put the car in drive and burned rubber as we screeched away. Several blocks later she calmed down and started to laugh. Now that we knew it was safe to do so, my sister and I joined in the laughter, too. Later we found a parking spot. Thankfully, it was a diagonal one. Each time we relived the incident in a hale of laughter, we agreed her failure was definitely the old man's fault! Mom's parallel parking skills had been challenged, but not diminished, from her perspective.

Despite her tendency toward being passive and modest, she also prided herself on her vocabulary. When she found a big word she was particularly proud of, she would taunt Dad by saying, "I have such pedantry. I bet you don't know the meaning of that word."

"Kids, listen. There your mother goes with another one of her fifty-cent words. She probably can't even spell it, but I bet I can," Dad would say as he proceeded to butcher the spelling no matter how many attempts he made.

Mom would reply, "Dad can't spell anything because he is German, and Germans try to spell everything exactly as it sounds."

I remember wondering if that was true, but Dad never disputed her comment, so I figured it was.

I didn't understand why, but it felt good to hear them tease each other. We could always tell when Dad was in a good mood because he referred to her as Mom, and she in return called him Dad. I assumed it was their attempt at tenderness. At those times, though rare, they sounded like the loving families I saw on television. I basked in the fantasy and welcomed the refuge from reality, but I was always waiting for Dad's mood to change. It happened so quickly, and so often, it was scary.

Now with Dad's illness, my phone conversations with Mom were no longer about the weather or local events like they had been in the past. The talk was always about illness, doctors, and medication. This morning her voice sounded tired and gravelly. Before, when she had a whiskey voice this early in the day, I would tease her by asking, "Have you been drinking?"

She would shout back with pretend disgust, "No, you silly girl!" and then we'd both laugh.

But this morning I knew alcohol wasn't the cause of Mom's raspy voice. I sensed even before she could explain that her voice was scratchy because she had been through a rough night with him. In hushed tones she told me that Dad was finally sleeping. She confirmed my suspicions as she described how he had slept very little during the night.

"Dad was up and down all night. He is having his headaches and stomachaches again," Mom explained. She thought it was probably his nerves. He'd had these same symptoms for years during stressful periods. "Poor Hooper. Dad must have kept her awake all night, too. She is passed out on the garage floor. Hasn't moved a muscle since I got up this morning," Mom said.

I smiled at the mention of Hooper. I could imagine her big, brown body and sad face looking up at Mom from where she was stretched out in exhaustion. She was a beautiful chocolate Labrador, and received no less attention and consideration from Dad than a human houseguest would be given in most homes. She was without a doubt my parents' four-legged baby.

"You know Hooper and Dad are clones of each other, Mom. If Dad has a headache, Hoop's got one too," I said to lighten the mood.

"You're right, sweetie. Well, I'm off to the beauty shop. I love you," she said.

As I maneuvered my way through the busy morning traffic, I thought about how much I missed Mom. She was a cute little thing, less than five feet tall, or 4'11" and ¾" as she steadfastly proclaimed.

Mom's light brown, very thin hair was one of her greatest sources of anxiety. She lived for her next permanent. In back of the daily diary she kept, she listed the date of each perm appointment. It was a big deal to her. Having been teased about her fine hair all her life, she was constantly in a state of flux of having just gotten a perm or of desperately needing a perm. And even though afterwards we could hardly tell the difference, we never let her know that.

Mom once read about a new product that would give body to limp hair. It was called Dippity-do. Not having extra money to buy it, Mom decided she could make her own. The end result was that gelatin is better mixed with fruit and refrigerated than used on one's hair for volume. Dad snickered at the results, and my sister and I belly laughed. Mom smelled good enough to eat, but her 'do was a disaster.

I recalled that my sister, who was just six years old, and I had just taken our seats on the school bus one day when she asked me, "Annie, what is a perm and why does Mom get them all the time?"

"A perm is when they curl Mom's hair. I heard her telling one of our neighbors that she gets them because her hair is so fine and thin. She thinks the perms will give her hair body."

"Body? What does that mean?" Julie asked.

I tried to explain it to her, even though I wasn't really sure, either. I just knew that each time Mom came home from her appointment, her hair smelled awful and looked even worse than before she left. I tried to talk Mom out of getting them, but she was an optimist when it came to her hair and was convinced the next perm would do the trick. Besides, she treated the trips to the beauty parlor like a social event. She put on a little makeup and even looked a little dressed up. Upon returning, she always had wild-looking curls and a little treat for my sister and me.

My ringing cell phone jarred me from the memory. "Hey, Mom. Thought you were headed to the beauty shop."

"I am, but I forgot to tell you that after my last perm was so bad, I have a new lady working on me today. Keep your fingers crossed for me. All I need is your dad feeling sick like he is and bad hair, too!" She giggled and said, "Gotta go. Love you, honey."

I laughed as I hung up the phone, realizing how true her words were. Bad hair and bad Dad would truly be a double whammy!

Chapter Eight

"Good morning, Annie. How are your parents doing? Are they excited you're coming home?" asked Christine, our office secretary.

"You know, sometimes when I talk to them, I think they are, and then during our next conversation I'm not so sure," I replied.

"Well, I'm keeping them and you in my prayers," Christine said as she placed her hands together as if praying.

The office chatter had brought me back from my daydreaming. It was another rainy morning in south Florida. We'd had over a week of the wet stuff, but we were used to it. It was, after all, hurricane season. As Midwesterners, we grew up with winter, spring, summer, and fall. Florida had only three seasons—tourist season, lobster season, and hurricane season.

Since it was Tuesday morning, the weekly mandatory office meeting was about to get underway with bagels in abundance and coffee flowing as freely as the voices in the conference room. Hesitant to start our workday, I and several of the other realtors lingered in the lobby watching the morning news on television. Then suddenly, normalcy as we knew it came to a screeching halt.

"Oh, my God. Did they just say a small plane crashed into the World Trade Center?" I asked my coworker who had just joined me. We continued to listen and learned that not one, but two commercial airplanes had just crashed into the World Trade Center in New York City.

Instinctively my thoughts went to the airline crew members and their families. One of my many jobs was as a flight attendant for Eastern Airlines. Any aviation story, especially a tragedy, always garnered my full attention. Each time I heard of an airline crash, it was a shocking realization that the efficacy of the safety training we received as flight attendants came down to a few desperate moments of recall and execution. Worse yet, in my case at least, that ability could have often been compromised by a layover hangover. I prided myself on never drinking on the job, but we called the time right after the flight our crew debriefing, and the location was always the hotel lobby bar.

Snagging an airline job had been a dream come true for me. Having survived only one miserable semester at a Bible college after high school, followed by a marriage gone sour to a man I hardly knew, I was stepping into a job I hardly knew anything about. I had taken many jobs unaware of the needed qualifications or the job description, but this was the most adventurous one yet. I remember writing on my airline application, "One of the reasons I want this job is because I love people and love to travel."

The truth was, what I really loved was the thought of leaving home. First, I had run away to the Bible college. Then I ran into a marriage with a classmate from high school. Both actions were colossal mistakes, made with immaturity and no forethought to consequences.

It had taken me three interviews, and actually not being invited to the third, to finally land the airline job. I was elated at the opportunity, hoping this attempt to flee would be successful. I could finally say goodbye to the Hoosier state dressed in a flight attendant uniform and looking out an airplane window.

Several weeks before my airline training started, I received a letter in the mail with an Eastern Airlines return address. My excitement was palpable. My parents listened as I read the letter aloud.

"*Congratulations on your acceptance into the Flight Attendant Training Class for Eastern Airlines. Upon graduation, your class will be based in Newark, New Jersey.*"

Although my parents and I didn't recognize it immediately, our small, rural world was about to get a lot bigger. Mom, Dad, and I stood in awkward silence at the back door where I had hurriedly torn open the letter. None of us wanted to be the first to admit we had no idea where Newark was!

Dad finally said, "I'll get the atlas."

Dad headed to the garage where he retrieved his atlas and we found Newark on the map. There he marked the site of my future home with a big black X. Dad could not hide his pride in me. I liked the feeling, but for some reason it also made me uncomfortable and embarassed like the airline had made a mistake, like I wasn't worthy. I retreated to my room and read the letter over and over.

As the morning news of the airplane hijackings and aftermath spread, the office lobby filled with employees gathering around the television. The images were beyond graphic. They looked like special effects from a movie. Many of us cried even though chances were slim that we knew any of the victims. But in a sense of community, like sheep in a flock, together we mourned for them as if they were family.

Within an hour the office was emptied and the doors were locked. Real estate didn't seem as important as it had a few hours before. We retreated to our homes and the endless hours of media coverage that followed, and began to absorb the sheer magnitude of the horrific event.

Earlier in the day, my mind had been consumed with thoughts of ailing parents and an impending trip scheduled to start in just three days. The grief I felt was heavy and dizzying, like nausea, and it was compounded by a nightmare I'd had two nights earlier.

Waking with a shudder and chills from a deep sleep, I was so frightened by the nightmare that I was unable to open my eyes. I had pulled the cover up over my head and lay in bed for some time. I could not remember the exact content of the dream, but there was no doubt it was traumatizing. I was paralyzed with fear and confusion. Later that day, I made an appointment with a counselor I had been seeing. After describing the incident to her, she summized that it might have come about because of the unease and anxiety of going back home. Her explanation seemed reasonable to me until the next morning—9/11. Was the dream a coincidence, or a premonition of the tragedy that had just occurred?

For this day, at least, my plans and worries about returning to my home of origin seemed minute and inconsequential as the dark particulars and human blood of September 11, 2001, seeped into and saturated our lives.

Chapter Nine

Life didn't feel quite normal after the morning of September 11, but there was work to be done and decisions to be made. There was cleaning out my desk, closing my checking and utility accounts, and worrying. And the following day, and the day after, there was more worry. I could hear the tiny voice of reason inside trying desperately to negotiate with the unreasonable part of me, but it was drowned out by the din of fear blaring in the childish part of my brain. I couldn't see that I was running again as I had done all my life from one uncomfortable situation to the next. Like an old nag with blinders on, my mantra of "I have to go" became my auto response.

I'm sure most of these concerns were on my mom's mind, too. During phone conversations, she asked many times, "Do you really think you need to come home? What about leaving your daughters? They're so young. Dad isn't feeling great, but we are doing okay. Have you thought this through, honey? I'm not sure it's a great idea."

"I need to be there, Mom." Even though I was thinking it, I didn't say you're still sick and now Dad is dying. "I'm not changing my mind. I'm coming home." I quipped again to friends and anyone else who would listen, "I have to go. They need me."

Then to my horror, following my repetitive response of "I have to go home," I heard myself repeating the words my dad used when his opinion was voiced and there was no room for negotiation—the very phrase I hated so much—"I have to go home. *End of story.*"

40

Emotion over intellect had me in its grip. This mental state caused me to conveniently forget that some things and some people aren't meant to be, nor do they always want to be rescued.

Chapter Ten

I don't recall the insane moment when I made the decision to take all my personal belongings with me to Indiana instead of storing them until my return. After all, I thought it was a temporary move even though my actions were not backing that premise.

As we shopped for packing boxes and tape, my daughter, Chelsea, asked, "Mom, you're bringing *all* your stuff with you?"

"That's my plan, hon."

I refrained from telling her the logic behind my decision, perhaps because there was no logic. Loaded in the truck I was renting would be all my stuff—everything I owned, including furniture, rugs, and an ironing board, even a little dirty laundry would be coming along with me. She seemed satisfied with my answer. She knew her grandma and grandpa were sick and that's all that seemed to matter to her right now.

Years later I would recall this conversation and realize all my stuff hadn't included my most precious possessions—my two daughters, ages twelve and fourteen.

I was in third grade. At nine years old, I was a shy, freckled-faced kid whose dad had just set our house on fire. Dad had come home very late, drunk as a skunk, and decided to cook for himself. While waiting for the skillet to heat, he passed out in a kitchen chair. Mom awoke to smoke and flames coming from the stove. My first memory of that night is Mom's shrill voice piercing the darkness as I rubbed my eyes trying to wake up.

"Girls, wake up. We have a fire. Gotta get you out of here," Mom said.

She picked up my sister, whose eyes were still closed, and grabbed my hand and pulled me along as we headed toward the back door. The night air was cold and it was so dark outside. The garage was separate from the house, and when we reached it, she put us both in the station wagon.

"Lock the doors, Annie, and don't get out until I come back. Okay, honey?" Before I could answer, she was gone. We watched as she ran back into the house. When she returned, she told us how grateful she was that she had managed to put out the fire herself without calling the fire department. Dad was nowhere to be seen when she brought us back to the house. I assumed Mom had put the drunk to bed like I'd seen her do before.

The charred smell of the fire lingered through most of the summer. It was in our clothes and our bedspreads, and I convinced myself I could even taste it in our toothpaste.

The next day Mom explained to us that it was just a bad-luck house. We'd had a bat fly through the chimney and into the living room, leaving us screaming and running for cover; Cubby, our family dog, was mauled to death by another dog in the backyard; using gasoline instead of starter fluid, Dad had blown up the brick grill he'd worked so hard to build; playing on a rope swing, my sister had fallen and broken an arm; my front tooth got chipped on a soda bottle; and Mom had fallen down a flight of stairs and into a window, leading to a trip to the emergency room where her bloody face and arms were treated.

The night after the fire, Julie asked as she crawled into bed, "Sister, do you think this is just a bad luck house like Mom said?" I didn't have an answer, but I did figure after that horrible day that things couldn't get any unluckier or worse. I was wrong. The bad luck continued.

We lived only two blocks from my elementary school so we often walked home for lunch. One day at lunchtime, it was announced on television that the president of the United States, John F. Kennedy, had been assassinated. The impact of the news didn't sink in until I walked back to school and found a note posted on the front door. "*School closed due to President's death.*" The words sent a chill through me and I ran all the way home. The next week we got more bad news. A vicious dog that lived near our school playground had jumped the fence and attacked a child who was playing on the swings. Now, we not only had a bad luck house, but a bad luck school as well.

The recollection of the bad luck house prompted me to ask myself a disturbing question. Was I about to become the parent creating bad luck memories for my children? I was, after all, about to abandon them and head off to another state. Was I acting like a parent to my children, or a child to my parents?

Chapter Eleven

Relationships are the Achilles heel of most alcoholics and addicts. I knew I suffered from this impairment as far back as I could remember, even years before I'd had my first alcoholic beverage.

In grade school, it was a tall, male skating instructor. In junior high, I found the target of my affection in a disc jockey at a radio station where I worked for a short time to fulfill a 4-H project. In high school, it was a crush on a math teacher. In each incident, I was drawn to an older man, usually one in authority and one, from my perspective, that made me feel special. The attraction was the attention I received. It filled a part of my soul that was empty. It was also dangerous and forbidden, and walking on the edge of my father's rigid boundaries. It made me feel alive, and then sad and ashamed. It was to become an ever-repeating cycle.

At the age of twenty-one when I had my first alcoholic drink, my unhealthy relationships became even more twisted and damaging. No longer were they girlish crushes and affections from afar. Now I found myself in drunken one-night stands and tormented entanglements. My mood swings were undeniable, and the unbridled sexual encounters brought on a deeper and deeper depression. And as usual in my life, there was no thought of repercussions or core values. Not once did I recognize the mood swings or the alcohol as a factor in my dispicable behavior. I fell down. I got up. I moved on.

During the first year of my recovery, I learned I had no idea how to form, and certainly not to sustain, a bond with another person, be it a man or a woman. I took you as a hostage in either a romantic relationship or just as a friend, and at some point, you were released when the emotional ransom had been paid and I was finished with you. Occasionally, I looked backward at the pile of dead soldiers I'd left behind, and with an air of aloofness, wondered what had happened.

Early recovery had not absolved me of the propensity to try to protect myself by eliminating others from my life with the precision of a weed whacker. Sobriety had started to make me painfully aware of my routine, and the work and discipline it would take to change it.

While trying to stay sober the first couple of months in the twelve-step fellowship, I'd met a real character named Don. I very clearly saw myself being drawn into the routine. First the attraction and flirtation, and then a sense of codependency grew because he had more time in sobriety than myself.

I'd never met anyone like Don before. Bald headed and tattooed with a thick Brooklyn accent, he was someone whose path I probably never would have crossed had it not been in the rooms of recovery. He was a jovial sort, full of stories and eager to tell them to anyone who would listen.

My girls met and loved him and his pirate laugh, as he teased and tickled them incessantly. I was taken by his sensitivity, and intrigued by the diversity of our backgrounds. Don had volunteered to be the chauffeur on my trip to Indiana. As I readily accepted his offer, I didn't know whether to laugh or cry when I thought of the possibilities of the reception he might receive at our destination.

In Fort Lauderdale, there was nothing unusual about Don's physical appearance, but in my hometown he would stick out like a penguin in the Amazon. Many folks, including my dad, were good at shoveling out grief to anyone who fell outside the Midwestern guidelines of what was normal. Those who grew beards, wore their hair long, or dared to display any expression of individualism were met with scowls and verbal barbs of belittlement and condescension behind their backs or right to their faces. In this case, if they could just get past Don's rough voice and exterior, they would discover that behind his bright blue eyes was a heart of gold.

Poor Don, I thought. He probably had no idea what he'd gotten himself into. He was such a good sport to help me out with the drive. Gas money and an airline ticket back to Florida was enough to convince him to join my sojourn. I was grateful he would be with me on the trip.

Chapter Twelve

The day of our departure arrived. It was humid for a
September day. The morning air was heavy with stickiness
and pollution. It was also heavy with sadness, sadness for our
country, and the same for my leaving family and friends. My nerves
were raw and my irritability level was off the chart. I was trying so
hard to capture a mental picture of my daughters that morning. They
dressed for school in their white blouses and blue plaid uniforms.
They hated and grumbled each time they had to put on their close-
toed black uniform shoes. When you have grown up in Florida as
they had, the only acceptable shoe is the flip-flop. Even though I
knew they would be in good hands with their father and our favorite
nanny, who had returned to us from Nicaragua during my stay in
treatment, my heart ached when I thought of how much I was going
to miss them while I was in Indiana.

On the drive to school they were unusually quiet and clingy.
Katie held tightly onto my hand, and Chelsea was sitting so close
she was nearly on my lap. I couldn't begin to imagine what kind of
thoughts were running through their little heads.

I knew they were trying to be brave for Grandma and Grandpa.
Wasn't that what I was trying to do, too? Wasn't bravery the reason
I was going? The news said the 9/11 tragedies were bringing people
and families closer together. It made me wonder if I was leaving my
family or going to my family. I was learning a new meaning of not
knowing whether you were coming or going. I felt trapped in the

middle, so I decided to follow the horrible advice I'd heard Dad offer up many times in the past. "Do something, even it's wrong."

We arrived in front of the school. The car circle helpers were there as they were every morning to assist kids quickly out of their cars and to keep the line moving. For everyone else it was just another normal school day—kids unloading with their hair still mussed, and backpacks and lunches hanging awkwardly from little shoulders far too small for such loads. But in our vehicle nothing felt normal. With an "I love you," a hug, and a deluge of tears, I waved good-bye and blew kisses to my two precious little red-headed girls.

"I'll see you soon, I promise," I yelled out the window.

"Tell Grandma and Grandpa hello for us," they yelled in unison. The last thing I saw was them blowing kisses in my direction.

I only made it a few blocks from the school when I had to pull over. I couldn't stop the tears. I made an attempt to console myself by saying out loud that I had made the right decision, but I was haunted by the sad and confused little faces of my daughters. Despite attempts to disregard the possible outcome, in my heart and because of childhood memories I was aware of the impact and scarring this kind of moment can leave on a child. I knew such a moment many, many years ago had scarred my little sister.

I was only in the first grade and too young to recognize how selective storytelling applied to the adults in my family. Sometimes we only hear half the story because the storytellers choose to only tell that part. Perhaps like many parents, mine made preemptive attempts at hiding the details of sordid human affairs they believed were beyond our comprehension. In truth, although we were children, the half-truths darted in and out of our peripheral consciousness like dust bunnies that travel from one corner of the room to the next, not quite in the open but never fully outing themselves. We were just kids, but we sensed the dishonesty. For us it morphed into mystery and insecurity when one night a dust bunny showed his real face and it was not a pretty sight. The tale of a sad little girl and her doll came to mind. It was the story of my sister's short-lived career as a hairdresser.

I was so proud of my pajamas with the feet attached. They were soft, pink fleece and covered in sock monkey images. All the monkeys were wearing red hats. I was not a happy camper on nights I had to wear anything else.

I was awakened by the sound of my mother's voice and her hand gently rubbing my arm. She said, "Get up, girls. We're going to Grandpa's house. We've got to go get Daddy."

I didn't know what time it was but I knew it wasn't time to get up for school. It was still dark outside and the house was so quiet. Mom didn't even make us put on our clothes. She gathered us up, and the next thing I knew we were in the car heading somewhere. My sister had her favorite doll tucked underneath her arm exactly the way she slept with it at night. She had named her doll Seetsie. We had no idea how she came up with that name, but she talked about and to Seetsie all the time.

The chilly night air gave me goosebumps and I was grateful for my sock monkey pajamas. My sister and I huddled together in the back seat and it wasn't long before we were sound asleep again, our earlier sudden awakening forgotten and the circumstances of our journey lost to slumber and the childhood ability to fall asleep anywhere.

When I awoke, it was to voices—angry voices. The light streaming through the car window caused me to squint. The car's engine was still running. The light was coming from my grandfather's porch where he and my mother were talking. My mom was waving her arms in the air. She looked angry. I noticed she wasn't wearing shoes. I wondered if her feet were cold. Why were we at grandpa's and where was Dad? The adults disappeared into the house.

Left alone, my sister and I got out of the car and headed into the house. We passed through the darkened living room and walked toward the kitchen where there was light. As we stood in the kitchen door, every face in the room turned to look at us. There was the sound of a gasp, and then the room turned frenetic with attempts to rush us out.

But they were too late. We had already seen the unimaginable for a child's eyes. Dad's was the only face that hadn't looked our way. He was still in his work clothes lying face-up on the kitchen floor. His whole head was bloody and so swollen I could only see one eye. The front of his shirt was torn open exposing the white undershirt I always saw him put on during cold weather. The undershirt was bloody, too. I noticed his fingernails were trimmed short. I don't why I noticed this, but I realized I had never really looked at them before. He didn't move. I thought maybe it wasn't really my dad. I felt lightheaded and nauseous like we did on playful summer afternoons when we would spin around in the yard until we were so dizzy we would fall down laughing.

"Oh, my God. Come on, girls. Back to the car," Mom barked, as she grabbed our hands and practically dragged us to the back door.

"You were supposed to stay in the car. Now get back in there and stay this time. I'll be out in a few minutes." Her voice was rough and heavy. I'd never heard that voice before.

"But Mom, what about Dad? What happened to him?" I asked.

"Don't worry about it, honey. He'll be all right." The old voice had returned. It was softer.

My sister and I sat in the back seat in silence as we watched Mom go back in. A little while later she came outside again, and this time took us back into Grandpa's house. The kitchen had been cleared of body and debris, and I could smell coffee brewing. Usually this smell early in the morning made me sick to my stomach, but for some reason the familiarity of the routine was comforting to me right now. Maybe I was unconsciously looking for normal and right now coffee brewing in the morning was the only normal I could find.

Mom took us to one of Grandpa's bedrooms and tried to make us comfortable enough to go back to sleep. My sister asked for her doll. Mom rubbed Julie's forehead and said, "I think you dropped her by the front door, honey. I'll look for her and bring her back to you in a little while. Now go back to sleep. Okay?"

Sleep? I couldn't even close my eyes. I listened for voices or any sounds coming from the other rooms. The rest of the night and the next day none of the adults spoke of my father. It was as if the image of him prostrate on the floor had been a scene from a bad movie or a fleeting nightmare. I was afraid to ask questions, and my sister was probably too young to even put things together, although it did have an impact on her as we would soon realize.

Later that morning, we stumbled upon the fate of my sister's doll, the one she was almost never separated from—the one with blue eyes, curly blonde hair, and tiny pink lips. She had been abandoned behind the sofa. Red marker scribbles, a perfect shade of blood red, marred her eyes and the rest of her little face, and all over her head were bare spots where big chunks of hair were missing. We all looked over at Julie. Mom gingerly picked up the doll and held it in her arms like a mother would hold a real baby.

"Julie, what happened to Seetsie?" Mom asked.

My sister didn't say a word. She looked down at the floor and crossed her arms over her chest like she did when she was angry or pouting.

"Honey, what happened to your doll?" Mom gently asked again.

My sister dropped her head to her chest and started to sob. Then she bolted out of the room as fast as her chubby little legs would take her. Mom followed her and the remaining adults began their futile attempts to restore Seetsie's face.

We found out later in the day that Julie had put the doll's head into a large commercial can opener Grandpa had mounted on the wall in the kitchen. She had given her a haircut and a face that looked like Daddy's.

Despite the adults' attempts, the ink on Seetsie's face wouldn't come off. It turned out to be indelible, just like the memories of that night. Seetsie would never be the same, and I doubted my sister and I would ever be the same, either.

Chapter Thirteen

I pulled up in front of my apartment and found Don waiting for me in our rented truck. It was 8:00 a.m. I knew in just a few minutes my girls would be standing up in their classrooms to recite the Pledge of Allegiance, and as they did so, I would be heading north out of the state.

I closed my eyes and again tried to ignore the pain. What will my absence do to my girls? I silently asked myself over and over. A panic spread over me and Don must have recognized it. I appreciated his tenderness but it couldn't stop the tears.

He reached out and took my hand, saying, "Everything will work out, Annie. Now, let's get this truck on the road!"

For a short time I forgot about my girls. But each time I would look down at my watch I realized they would soon be going to lunch, then gym class, and then home and I wouldn't be there. This grim reality haunted me for the remainder of the day as Don and I rolled through the state of Florida.

Similar to a bride-to-be's focus and ensuing chaos of planning a wedding and never really thinking about *being* married, my thoughts had been consumed with preparing for the trip and not the trip itself, nor the destination. I wondered if instead of a bride-to-be it made me a martyr-to-be.

"Don, do you think I'm making a mistake going home?" I asked as our truck moved along the interstate. As I was often guilty of, I asked questions not looking for the truth, but for words of affirmation.

Don chose the safe way out when he replied, "I think it's a little late to think about that now, Annie."

I didn't like that response so I told myself the question probably didn't have a good answer anyway—similar to a wife asking her husband, "Honey, does this dress make me look fat?"

Holding my breath and alternating between prayers and swears each time I heard an unusual sound coming from underneath our truck, the miles ahead felt daunting. I was waiting for the truck to break down at any moment.

As we left the familiar behind, the news of 9/11 came along with us. Each hour that passed brought us a clearer awareness of the enormity of the tragedy. As we drove, we began to see the pain firsthand springing up in front of us like political candidate signs that dot the roadsides during an election year. We saw prayers on billboards, memorials to lives lost on bank signs, and patriotic words painted in red, white, and blue across car and store windows. The pain was everywhere.

On the truck radio, Don and I listened to cell phone calls from the doomed airplanes that had been placed minutes, even seconds, before the plane crashes. The calls were sickening and riveting at the same time. We tried turning off the radio, but like the impulse to look at road kill when you don't want to look at it, we felt compelled to listen to the details of what we really didn't want to hear. The public speculation and endless gruesome details of the attacks proved to be insidiously addictive, especially for two recovering alcoholics like myself and my chauffeur.

And still my mind darted back and forth between this catastrophic situation and the unsettling one we were driving toward in Indiana. I wondered what Dad's thoughts were on the terrorist attacks. I could just imagine his rage and tirades. Of course there was the possibility that he wasn't keeping up with the news, but surely he wasn't that sick.

Mom and Dad were probably counting the minutes until my arrival, right? I closed my eyes and took a deep breath, wrestling with the uncertainty of what lay ahead. I had a lot of unanswered questions. How bad was Dad's condition? Would my Mom be able to handle this? She was a follower, not a leader, and we all knew she'd never been the same since her colon surgery. She was physically weaker, and her cognitive skills often appeared to be diminished. We had always teased her about her poor memory but it was worse now, and she often seemed to be confused and flustered by the simplest request or activity.

My worries were occasionally interrupted by an outburst of laughter from Don as we passed city limit signs for one small burg after another. Often "Welcome to" and "Thank you for visiting" signs were less than a half mile apart from each other. The majority were tiny towns with one or two stoplights at the most. And I had forgotten about the keen sense of humor many Southerners have when they name their little towns.

Welcome to Hopeulikit, Georgia.

City limits of Bugtussle, Kentucky.

Several times Don jarred me from a trance when he yelled, "Oh, my God! Look at that name!"

"Don, if you think that name is funny, how about my maiden name? Imagine what a drag childhood can be with a family name like Limp and a home address in Whiteland. There were so many Limps in the area where we lived that I seriously never even thought of the name being unusual until I was an adult and an airline captain pointed it out one day in a very unusual and embarrassing way. It is standard procedure before flights for the crew to go to the cockpit and introduce themselves to the captain of the aircraft. I remember vividly that I was flying on a three-day trip with another flight attendant named Carol Clapp. I entered the cockpit and said, 'Good morning, Captain.'

He turned around to look at me and with a deadpan face said, 'Good morning. Which one are you? Limp or Clapp?' A little timidly I replied, 'My name is Annie Limp.' He shook his head slowly and finally broke into a smile as he said, 'Damn! With one you can't and with one you wish you hadn't!'"

Don let out one of his pirate laughs and then asked, "Did you understand what the pilot was talking about?"

"Ha ha. Of course I did. I'm not that much of a country bumpkin. I was shocked though."

It was the first time I had comprehended the grief and teasing my father, his three brothers (aka the Limp boys), and an uncle who owned a plumbing business with the same last name must have experienced their entire lives. Limp Plumbing, Limp Electric and Limp Nursing Home were just a few of the local businesses proudly displaying our handle.

Don exclaimed, "Let me get this right. Instead of saying never mind keeping up with the Joneses, in your neighborhood it was watch out for those Limps!"

"That's right," I said as I punched him in the arm.

Much to my feigned chagrin, Don called me Ms. Limp the rest of the day.

Chapter Fourteen

Another five hundred miles closer to our destination, and just like the family cat usually one step ahead of the neighbor's dog, we left the summer heat several states behind in our exhaust. I rolled the truck window down. The aroma of autumn air and freshly cut grass made me smile. It was starting to smell like home, and the smell of home opened the dam on memories of a childhood in a rural area.

I was proud to be moving on into the fifth grade and excited about the new school year. Our family had just moved from the suburbs to a new place in the country and, of course, to a new school. On our first trip to see our new house, my sister and I were delighted to find that Mom and Dad had forgotten to tell us about the treasure awaiting us in the backyard. We didn't care what the rest of the house looked like once we discovered the old, wooden outhouse in the backyard of our new place. These dilapidated structures dotted the countryside. We'd often seen them on drives through the country, but we'd never owned one of our own. And this one was a beauty—a two-seater and dry as a camel in the desert because it hadn't been used in years.

My sister and I immediately thought "clubhouse." It did not need to be large or sophisticated. If it could be glued, nailed, or shoved together, we'd try to make a clubhouse out of it. It was our passion. We'd had an assortment of creative refuges. We'd used a commercial parachute as an outside sleeping shelter, a poorly constructed tree house for a hideout, and a combination of a double roll of wire fencing stuffed with cut grass from a pasture as an igloo-type structure. Now we had a two-star, two-seater clubhouse for real. My sister and I were beyond delighted. Once we got back in the car, Dad didn't waste a second before he started teasing us about our new two-seater outhouse.

"Hmmm, a two-seater. What happens if there's a family of six and everyone has to go at the same time?" he asked us while barely containing his laughter. "Hey, girls, I've got an idea for a sign for your new clubhouse. On the door it should say, 'No ONE allowed, and that means you, TWO!' Get it? Number one and number two!"

Though he hadn't shared many details of his childhood with us, we did know that some people still used outhouses when he was a kid. In vivid detail he'd described how he and some school friends would wait until they saw an outhouse was occupied and then sneak up and tip it over with the occupant still inside! No matter how many times he repeated it, we thoroughly enjoyed this story, but only half as much as he enjoyed telling it. We figured we'd be hearing about our two-seater for many years to come.

Dad also had a fascination with a red barn in the area. Several miles from our house our travels often took us past a huge, wooden red barn. Most homes in the country had barns, so there was nothing unusual about it except that this one was perfectly round in shape. You could bet the farm that Dad would chime in each and every time we passed it, "Did you hear the story about that barn? A man went crazy in there trying to find a corner to pee in." It was a little sick but we all waited for that line and laughed in spite of ourselves. We started to look forward to passing that unusual barn. It was as close to a family tradition as we had back then.

Once I complained to Mom about our not having any family traditions. With feigned indignance, she claimed we certainly did have some traditions. She was particularly proud of the frisking tradition.

A how-to on frisking your dad probably shouldn't have been a childhood lesson, but there were many instances where humor possibly kept us from losing our minds, and this tradition certainly was humorous and unusual. The frisking involved rolling Dad, and it became one of the few upsides to his drinking. While Dad was passed out on the floor or in a chair, Mom taught us the fine art of getting what you want when the giver is unaware of what's going on. We would wait until we were fairly sure Dad was completely comatose with intoxication. Then Mom would make her move as my sister and I hovered nearby. The positioning of his pants pockets was crucial. If he was lying on the pocket containing his wallet, our game plan was to make him stir just enough to move him into another position exposing the right pocket. Sometimes this took several attempts, and we would jump with fear when it looked like we had gone too far and he might be waking up. Mom was steadfast, though, as she got him to roll a little to the left or right all the while trying to hold back giggles.

Dad wasn't exactly stingy with his money, but he wasn't generous, either, so these 'rolls' were our only chance to get extra loot. After all, he would be passed out and we knew he would have no idea what had been left in his wallet from his escapades the night before. When he woke up, he would count the bills and wonder where and how he had spent all his cash, but embarrassment would prevent him from making any public inquiries or accusations in our direction.

Once he was in a perfectly exposed position, Mom would gingerly slide Dad's wallet out from his pocket with the agility and grace of Houdini getting out of a straitjacket. We would then scamper to a back bedroom where we alternately squealed with joy and counted the bills with delight. There were occasional flickers of guilt for rolling Dad, but they were quickly nudged out by the excitement of planning how to spend the money.

It was also a pleasant discovery to find out Dad hid his money everywhere. Maybe it was the farmer in him, but he didn't totally trust banks. He let them hold some of his funds, but the majority he squirreled away in secret little spots all over the property. Finding Dad's stash turned into a game for us. When Mom ran low on funds, and Dad wasn't forthcoming with some cash, we did the hunt for bucks. Common hiding spots were in little nooks and compartments in the barn—a couple hundred in a toolbox, a couple hundred in his seed drawer. You could always count on several hundred in the egg bin or butter compartment of the refrigerator. My sister and I decided that's where the term cold cash came from.

Mom was careful never to take the whole amount we found. "We'll just pilfer a little off the top. He'll never notice," she would say to us with a smile and shaky assurance. She sounded experienced and knowledgeable, so we figured she knew about the important things a mother should teach her daughters, like taking care of money matters regardless of whose cash it was.

Don was cursing at the traffic, which had come to a complete stop, but my storytelling didn't subside. And when I finally took a breath, Don looked over at me and asked, "How the hell do you remember all these things? I think you should write a book!"

"Hmm, maybe I will someday. And when I'm a famous, rich author, I'll hire you to be my full-time chauffeur," I said with the best air of uppityness I could muster.

Chapter Fifteen

W e hit the road early on the last morning of our trip. Showered and caffeinated, we left our motel rooms and headed out toward our wheels. I pictured myself as a trucker loading up my rig for another haul. I shared this vision with Don, and he teased me with the words, "No trucker would make any money if they needed to stop as many times as you do. Tell me about your folks, Annie You haven't said much about them except that they are sick."

"Well, my dad is a walking, talking *Farmer's Almanac*. Don't suppose you've ever read that publication, right?"

"The *Farmer's Almanac*? No, it wasn't exactly required reading in Brooklyn," Don answered. "Lots of thugs and mafia, but not many farmers in those neighborhoods."

I could picture my dad emerging from his bedroom as he read, "'When the wisteria blooms early, you will have cold and rainy spring weather.' See? I told you. Forget the local weatherman. You can depend on the good ol' *Farmer's Almanac*. They're always right on the money. Every time. End of story." That would be Dad's proclamation for the morning.

I explained to Don, "As sure as Sunday morning meant Mom frying cornmeal mush, you could bet Dad was reading the *Farmer's Almanac* right after he finished his newspaper. You could also bet your Sunday best that Dad would be voicing an opinion on everyone and everything he read. He would sit on his soapbox, also known as the couch, and educate anyone within hearing distance. He believed a farmer's words were as good as the Gospel. Other than his own opinion, none was held with more regard than that of the *Farmers Almanac*. End of story."

"Can you still buy this *Farmer's Almanac*, and what else is in it?" Don asked.

I explained that it was still published, and the information varied from weather forecasts to naming children after flowers and ordering seeds from the oldest seed company in America.

"Farmers and country people use the almanac to determine just about everything for the coming year, including the weather. It's crazy but that's how it is. I'm sure Dad has a few old copies stacked in the barn that he would be glad to give to you, Don," I said with a chuckle.

Don was quick to reply, "No, that's okay, I was just wondering. It's a miracle I've survived all these years without reading it!"

"Better not let Dad know that, or he will be sending some home with you, that's for sure!" I replied. As I gazed out the truck window, I said, "As old as I am, I can still hear my dad's words from my childhood ringing in my ears. He said, 'Farmers don't trust anyone who wears a bow tie or sunglasses. You'll never see a farmer in sunglasses. They don't trust anyone who wears 'em. I don't trust 'em either. Farmers are just like dogs. Dogs can sense whether people are good or bad. It's something about the smell. They can smell a scoundrel right away. Dogs don't like people in bow ties or sunglasses either. Mark my words.'"

Don and I both laughed as he lifted his sunglasses from his eyes and winked at me.

Then I continued to explain, "My sister and I were little so we always listened, but I felt a quiet uneasiness about whether Dad knew what he was talking about. But he sounded so sure, he didn't leave us much room for doubt, and certainly no room for discussion. He spoke, and again that was the end of the story—no discussion wanted or needed."

Don's cell phone rang and he took the call, leaving me alone for a while with my thoughts. To this day, regardless of its validity, I still found myself sometimes staring at people who wore sunglasses. And my uninvited and unbridled contempt toward neckwear both disturbed and amused me. I could hear my dad's words as clear as the sky when I observed a man in a bow tie parking his car in a church lot. A God-fearing man wearing a bow tie? Obviously, he wasn't aware of the no bow tie code of morals that my dad and the entire canine world were aware of. I smiled at the thought.

Chapter Sixteen

Don seemed to be enjoying my stories and it helped pass the time, so I continued the walk down the Limp history lane.

"Did I tell you about the creek we lived by when I was growing up?" I asked.

Don shook his head no. "It was called Sugar Creek."

"Living next to the water sounds like fun," said Don.

"Well, yes and no," I said as I shrugged my shoulders and stared out the window.

I continued to be amazed that my sister's phone call could so easily and quickly pull me backward, creating a time warp that was both confusing and overwhelming. My mind wandered back to the good and bad of childhood where Sugar Creek was both my friend and my enemy.

"Well, we've got a little time to kill here, so tell me about the good and the bad parts." Don laughed.

"The good parts? Hmm. The creek's banks were blanketed in colors only nature could provide. I remember that the colors I saw there made the ones I saw in the crayon boxes look dull. The ground cover was a brilliant shade of green, and speckled with sunlight and deep blue blooms. Mom called the flowers bluebells. I wondered if she just made up that name, but they were beautiful. I can still see them as if it were yesterday. The area was mostly shaded, and the air was heavy with the smell of damp soil. Moss had taken hold on downed tree limbs, and the sweet, subtle fragrance of the bluebells rose from beneath the overgrowth. I'm telling you, Don, the combination of those smells offered a sensory delight like I had never experienced before. Come to think of it, it was my first smell of perfume with no ornate packaging or price tag. It was a smell I've never forgotten."

I didn't even know if Don was still listening until he said, "Too bad you couldn't have bottled that scent. You could be a millionaire right now, riding in a limo instead of this lovely rented truck! All right. Give it to me. The bad parts." He winked at me.

"The bad parts—those were the floods," I said as I closed my eyes, forcing myself back to that place, to the sounds and the feel of a childhood there.

I'd heard some people say they remember their own birth. I didn't. My earliest childhood memories were of the darker personality of Sugar Creek and the floods. The road we lived on was one of the narrow two-lane country ones where there is no shoulder and no room for driving errors. One inch too far to the right and you and your car were in the ditch. The earth sloped down on both sides of the road at an almost 90-degree angle from the edge of the pavement. A steep gravel driveway led down to our place. It was a small, simple, white house with a green-shingled roof and an open, unpaved carport where my sister and I made mud pies and held in Mason jars the fireflies we'd caught the night before. There didn't seem to be extra dollars for toys, so we played with what nature gave us and what our imaginations could create. As we grew older and found ourselves bored, Dad would say to us, "Go play on the railroad tracks." We didn't take him seriously but thought it was an odd thing for an adult to say.

Sugar Creek was to the east, the roads to the north, and both south and west sides were flanked with a densely overgrown wooded area. Our little house sat in the middle of the property like it had been dropped into the center of some sort of sinkhole.

"I'm telling you, Don. That creek gave my sister and me nightmares."

"How often did the creek flood?"

"Every time it rained hard."

I told him a story about the morning we woke after a solid week of rain and found the creek had overflowed her banks and was well onto our property.

"What did you guys do when that happened?" he asked.

"Each time was different, but never pleasant," I replied.

I recalled one particularly disturbing night when the creek got high. We woke up on another stormy morning to our sixth day of rain. I'd overheard Mom and Dad talking about the chances of a flood. I heard Dad say, "The old creek has had just about more rain than she can handle."

By the end of the day, our house was completely surrounded by creek water and it was still raining. The basement windows were already underwater and Cubbie, our dog, sat pensively on the top step of the stairs that lead to our enclosed front porch. There were just two steps between him and the murky brown water that continued to rise at what my mom called a God-awful rate. After many frantic phone calls during the afternoon, Mom still couldn't find Dad, so she called Grandpa for help. My sister and I were still in our pajamas when Grandpa's green pickup truck slowed down and parked on the road above us because the water was too deep to drive in. He waded down to the house and carried us out one by one. I'd heard a lot of people talk about Grandpa and his obsession for the color green. Not only had he painted the outside of his truck his favorite color, but also the hubcaps, the steering wheel, and even the antenna. Dad said, "Grandpa will probably be buried with green paint still on his glasses."

Once we were all in the truck, I asked Grandpa if we could take Cubbie with us, too.

"No. Let's let him stay here. The water won't get much higher and he'll be more comfortable in his own yard. That dog's a survivor. He'll be just fine."

I usually trusted Grandpa, but this didn't seem like the right thing to do as we pulled away and I looked back where Cubbie sat watching us go. As I felt the truck start to move, I could feel the sting of tears coming. I watched out the window until I couldn't see our dog anymore.

It seemed like hours later when Dad showed up at Grandpa's house. I could tell Dad had been drinking and that he and Grandpa were having words. I overheard Grandpa saying, "Dammit, son. Where the hell have you been? In a bar, I suppose. Everyone's been trying to reach you. The creek's been coming up for hours. We looked all over town for you."

I heard Dad bellow from the kitchen, "Oh, it's just another damn flood. You people all panic. How many of these have we been through? This flood won't amount to more than a pinch of owl shit in the bottom of the ocean." As he pulled his coat on he grumbled, "Why would you leave Cubbie there? I'm going back to get him."

Dad was always spouting off one of his crazy sayings like the one about the owl shit. "It's not worth a pinch of owl shit in the bottom of the ocean." He was either angry and annoyed when he did this, or in a happy mood. You could never predict which it would be. He was famous for the line "Your ass sucks canal water!" I hadn't ever seen a canal, and I doubted Dad had either. None of us knew what he meant and none of us had the courage to ask. They were just Dad's sayings and we all listened without any understanding of where the words came from or what they meant.

Dad loaded up the rowboat in the back of his old, weathered gray panel truck and drove back to get Cubbie. Dad hadn't been available to rescue us, but we were sure happy he was at least there to save the dog.

I continued my Sugar Creek story to Don. "I guess my sister and I were typical five and seven year olds with a tendency to be drawn to and embellish the dramatic. With the house dark and quiet at night, the creek provided a soundtrack of eerie noises for us. I remember us pulling the bedcovers over our heads and talking in hushed tones into the night until sleep would finally overtake our boundless imaginations. Dad adored the creek. Any time we complained about how scary the creek was, Dad dismissed our concerns with a casual attitude.

"Sometimes at night my sister and I would look out our bedroom window and spot Dad down at the creeks's edge in black rubber hip boots, hunting cap, and flannel shirt doing what he called gigging for frogs. It was so dark there were times when we could only make out his profile. He said the frogs were best at full moon. With my childish reasoning, I couldn't imagine why anyone would want frog legs. Dad said they were good eatin'. I thought that was gross. Besides, eating them wasn't the thing on my mind. I was fretting over the miserable existence of those poor, legless frogs. I remember asking him why would a frog care if the moon is full?

"'It's in the *Farmer's Almanac*, like I've told you guys before. Those guys don't lie,' Dad would reply confidently. 'Everything in the world moves according to the moon's cycles. Ask your Mom about weaning baby animals and the cycles of the moon. It's all connected and it's right there in the almanac. If the wooly worms are furry and dark in the fall, we have a heck of a winter ahead of us. Thin and light colored means the winter will be mild. That book's more accurate than the Bible,' he would shout as he headed out the back door, letting the screen door slam behind him even though he was always scolding us for doing the same. No one dared say a thing to him about it. We all knew Dad played by his own rules."

After hearing my story, Don said to me, "But, Annie, don't you think that's the way most fathers are?"

"I don't know, Don. There was just something about that man. As I got older, I guess I started to question the validity of his beloved almanac. I attacked and challenged his beliefs. He defended his views, and so on and so on. Then the next day at school during a discussion with a fellow student or teacher, my fervor would give way to bewilderment as I found myself heralding his and the almanac's position—the same one I had been refuting just hours before. It was really confusing, and it certainly didn't make me feel good about myself. I didn't understand how he had that power over me. It still bothers me after all these years. Can you believe that?"

"I can, because I've felt the same way before. Sometimes the characteristics you love about a person are the same ones you hate," Don said.

"That's exactly it. It has taken me years to discern this oddity. How did you get so smart?" I asked Don, as I punched him in the arm.

"Hey! No physical abuse here. I'm the one transporting your junk. A little respect, please!" Don teased.

I didn't mention it to Don, but I couldn't count the number of times I remembered hearing myself defend my final opinion in some debate with Dad's ever famous words, "End of story." And immediately following, my next thought was always, "Oh, my God. I have turned into my Dad."

"Hey, Don," I said, "I hate to tell you but..."

He interrupted me. "Let me guess. We need another pit stop!"

"Yep."

After the bathroom stop and the purchase of assorted junk food and energy drinks, we were underway again. I gave up on finding a comfortable sitting position. I was constantly squirming. After several days on the hard, vinyl bench seat offered by the rental truck I decided comfortable just didn't exist in this vehicle.

"Don, I keep meaning to ask you. Have you ever been to Indiana before?"

Raising one eyebrow, he answered, "You kidding? I've never even heard of the place before!" He laughed and the sound reminded me of a character in a movie. He *was* a character.

Chapter Seventeen

Nineteen road hours and 1,155 miles later, just minutes before my bottom permanently become one with the seat and just as the sun was starting its descent, we pulled into the long concrete driveway I knew so well. It was like an out-of-body moment. Someone was arriving, but it wasn't me. I felt like I was watching the scene from a distance. It was surreal. Several times I caught myself holding my breath and had to consciously think about breathing in and out. Nausea and lightheadness came over me in waves.

Don was muttering something about where to park the truck, but I didn't comprehend anything he was saying. I was looking all around, taking in everything at once. It had been almost a year since I'd been to visit. Mom and Dad's house looked just as I remembered it, although somewhat smaller, like most things do when reality meets the image you've created from memory.

It was a simple ranch-style brick house, well manicured and modest. The white barn where I hoped to store my belongings sat at the end of the driveway next to the garden area. The many trees Dad loved so much—pines, apples, and maples—shaded the meticulously manicured lawn that stretched out to nearly an acre of land. I loved the grass. I loved the fresh smell of it. It was real grass unlike the weeds we had growing in Florida.

Don was still yakking but my attention remained elsewhere. My eyes continued to travel over each landmark, including the familiar round concrete patio with the red-stained picnic table Dad had built himself flanked by the old sliding glass doors that led to the living room. And next to the doors, barely tall enough to see over the sill, I spotted my mom where she was undoubtedly leaning against the kitchen sink and gazing out the kitchen window just as I had seen her do so many times. Jarred from her faraway look, my mom's eye met mine and her small, contemplative face broke into a smile.

"Annie, you're home!" she screamed as she ran from inside the house. "I've been pacing for hours and watching the driveway. Oh, honey, it's so good to see you."

Mom threw her arms around me. She was wearing her usual button-up-the-front cotton shirt and the same funky little cotton flat shoes we had teased her about since the day she brought them home from Walmart, or Wally World as her and Dad called it. Even the smell of her felt familiar. It was a mixture of Juicy Fruit gum and tobacco.

"Mom, you remember Don from your visit to Florida, don't you?" I said as I encouraged Don in her direction.

"Sure I do. Hi, Don. It's good to see you again. How did this child talk you into this trip?" she asked him as she reached out to give him a hug.

Dad must have heard the commotion. He emerged from his bedroom looking a little disheveled and I guessed he'd been taking a nap. Dad's shadow, Hooper, followed close behind him.

"Dad, I'm sorry. Did we wake you?" I asked.

He hadn't heard my question and yelled, "Well, there's no doubt Annie's home! You can hear that voice into the next county!"

I went to hug the old fart, a nickname we had given him years ago, and as I put my arms around him, I was shocked by how thin and frail he felt. Gone was his solid frame and spry step. His face was drawn and his voice was scratchy. I made a conscious attempt to keep from staring at him. Any doubts about coming home I might have harbored vanished as I watched him lower himself onto the picnic table seat.

Mom, graying and much thinner than the last time I'd seen her, appeared even shorter than usual. When I mentioned her decreasing vertical status, she smiled and retorted, "That's impossible, child! You don't get any shorter than I am!"

Our hellos and hugs felt restrained and awkward as we made small talk about the trip. Out of the corner of my eye I could see Dad sizing up my traveling partner, no doubt struggling to be cordial with him. Once again, I hoped beyond hope and despite previous experience, that he would be able to look beyond Don's physical appearance and see the kind, generous person he was.

"Is this your first time to Indiana, Don?" Dad asked.

"Yes, sir, it is," Don replied.

As he answered Dad's question, I saw him glance toward our neighbor's field. His face contorted into a combination of awe and fear. We all followed his gaze and realized he was watching a bull grazing in a nearby pasture.

Don's reaction sliced right through the tension when he pointed to the field behind us and said, "Remember, I'm from Brooklyn, so please don't judge me." He pointed to the black and white occupant of the field and said, "Is that a REAL bull no more than fifty feet from us?"

The city slicker made us all laugh. For a moment we forgot all about cancer.

Chapter Eighteen

I awoke the next morning in another world. There were no girls to wake up, no job to hurry off to, and no humidity. I could also smell coffee, and I hadn't been the one to make it. This couldn't possibly be Florida.

I found Dad sitting outside at the picnic table with his iced tea and his head in the newspaper. It was the local paper the *Daily Journal*. He was always complaining it had nothing in it as he shook the thin, five-page rag in the air. Nevertheless, he never missed a day of reading it.

"Morning, Dad," I chirped as I joined him outside.

"Hey, Annie, you're up early. How'd you sleep?" he asked as he handed the newspaper my way.

"Like a log, thanks. The trip wore me out. I guess Don's still asleep."

"Oh, no he isn't. He got up shortly after I did. Last time I saw him he was wandering around out back by the barn. He seems in awe of being in the country. Has he ever been outside of the city?" Dad asked.

I asked myself if Dad's face was wearing a look of doubt or sarcasm. After all these years, I still couldn't read him.

"He probably hasn't been out of the city much. Did he tell you he's from Brooklyn, New York? He's got an incredible story," I said.

"He did mention Brooklyn. How did he end up in Florida? Is he part of that program you're in?" Dad asked.

"Alcoholics Anonymous. Yep, that's where I met him. He's been sober about fifteen years. I think he came to Florida for his addiction treatment. What do you think of him?" I asked with the trepidation one might feel when asking the doctor for a medical diagnosis.

"He seems like a nice guy. Different, but nice. I don't get the tattoos though. Why does anyone on God's green earth do that? It's so damn ugly. Did I ever tell you that is the one thing my mom made me promise when I left for the Navy? She didn't want me to get any tattoos, which a lot of the guys did. I never got one because of mom's words."

"Yeah, I remember that story, Dad. I also remember your words when I wanted to get my ears pierced. You said, 'If God wanted you to have two more holes in your head, he would have given them to you!' Boy, did that make me mad. Mom pierced at least three or four of my friends' ears before I finally talked her into doing mine. Then we hid it from you for months!"

"Oh, you just thought you were hiding it. I knew all along," he said.

"You did not! You would have croaked!" I retorted. I spotted Don walking toward us from the barn. I yelled, "Morning there, city slicker!"

He raised his hands in the air acknowledging his new title and yelled, "That I am. Can't deny it!"

Mom cooked us up a good old-fashioned Hoosier breakfast of sausage and biscuits and fried mush. Don had never heard of mush so we explained it was just cornmeal mixed with water that had been refrigerated. Unfamiliarity with the dish obviously didn't bother him as he dug in and followed our lead by putting ketchup on half of the slices of mush and syrup on the other half. There was also a plate of sliced tomatoes from Dad's garden. He said they would probably be the last of the season. I explained to Don how very proud Dad was of his tomato crop every year. I later found out Don didn't even like tomatoes, but he ate them like a champ.

Don spent the day getting to know my parents. They were strangers to Don, and in many ways to me as well. It felt like it had been years since I had been home. As they answered his questions, I realized I was as intently listening to their answers just as he was. It made me realize that over the years most of our family conversatons were about the weather or the neighbors. We didn't talk much, if at all, about emotions.

"How long are you staying, Don?" Dad asked.

Don laughed as he looked over at me and said, "Well, now that I have safely delivered my cargo, I will be heading out tomorrow after I return the rental truck. I have an early morning flight."

Mid morning I spotted Dad and Don out in the garden. "Mom, do you see where they are? Don's probably never seen vegetables still in the soil."

"Your dad and his garden. He goes out there at least three or four times a day. Sometimes I see him just standing still in one of the rows like he's watching the plants grow. Of course Hooper loves it, too, especially when Dad picks her a ripe tomato. You know, she can carry one in her mouth all the way back to the house and never even break the skin. It's the soft mouth the Labradors have. I've no doubt Dad will show you how she does it before long. He shows everyone. Says she's the smartest dog he has ever had, just like he's said about every other dog we've ever had."

"Guess that runs in the family. I do recall at Christmas time you are the one who always says, 'It's the prettiest tree we've ever had!'" I said as I put my arm around Mom's shoulder and squeezed her. "It's so good to be home, Mom. I've missed you. Has Dad said anything about my coming home?"

"Not much, hon. A few concerns about you leaving your girls and your job. And he was adamant about not bringing your cats with you. I was scared to death you would bring them anyway. He would have blown his stack if you had."

"Well, despite your warnings, I almost did bring them. I figured once I got here with them, he would get over it. The only reason I didn't bring them was I realized there wasn't any room for them in the cabin of the truck. It wasn't until the last minute that I made other arrangements."

"You know, you're lucky to have an ex-husband that is kind enough to take in your animals while you're gone. I'm so glad you didn't bring them, Annie. Your dad was serious. There would have been hell to pay if you'd shown up with them," Mom said.

I shrugged my shoulders as I walked away and said, "Nah. He would have gotten over it." But I was thinking to myself that I hadn't really even paid any attention to Dad's protests. As I breathed a sigh of relief that I hadn't brought the furballs, I could hear my sponsor's voice saying it was time I started to realize that other people's boundaries and rules were not mine for changing or breaking. She referred to it as "part of the growing up process." Obviously, it was still a lesson I needed to work on.

The end of our first day turned out to be a beautiful fall night and I talked Mom and Dad into a bonfire. One of my fondest memories as a child were the evenings sitting around a fire and shooting the shit, as Dad would say. The fare on the menu was always hotdogs and marshmallows.

Weiner roasts, as we called them, were a passage of summer living at our house. Dad was constantly adding to a growing pile of wood and other combustible scraps out back behind the barn. This was the designated area for our roasts where we sat on logs, marveled at the fire, and ducked from the curling trails of smoke.

Dad wouldn't hear of buying store-bought roasting sticks. He cut small twigs from trees, cut the bark off, and chiseled one end to a point. We used these for roasting, and when in a pinch, we used wire coat hangers bent to accommodate our burnt hotdogs and flaming marshmallows, which we lovingly made into 'smores or Angels on Horseback by squeezing them between graham crackers and chocolate.

Don and I sat near the fire while my parents were in the house preparing to bring the food out.

"I haven't seen stars like this in a long, long time," Don said as he leaned backward, surveying the vast cloudless sky above us. "It's very peaceful here. I'm glad I got to come with you."

"I'm glad, too, Don. It's nice having you here because it eases a little of the awkwardness I feel with Dad. He hasn't said anything nasty yet, but I'm on edge waiting for the moment when he does."

Here I sat many years later in the same spot where on cool, clear sky nights, Mom and Dad had always sat around a fire with my sister and me. It was always a weiner roast but they seldom ate dinner with us. I remembered this had always bothered me. Now, maybe because of my own sobriety, it dawned on me that they probably didn't eat because the food would have killed their beer buzz. The first night here and already a childhood mystery had been solved.

As he always had, Dad built a beautiful fire. As we watched the embers glow, we introduced Don to the fine art of browning the dog without charring it. As the air cooled, the fire and the conversation warmed, and we reminisced on weiner roasts through the ages.

Long before the fire died out, Mom and Dad called it a night. They said they had expended all their energy worrying about Don and me driving and waiting for our arrival. We hugged and said good night. I watched them walk off through the yard and to the house.

79

Don said, "You look a little pensive. What are you thinking about, kiddo?"

"Not sure I'm thinking at all," I replied. "I feel kind of numb. So much has changed and yet nothing has changed. I'm a little scared. What have I gotten myself into here?"

Don and I remained with the fire in silent contemplation for what seemed like a good while before Don broke the silence.

"I have to tell you, Annie, after hearing your stories about your dad, I was pretty nervous to meet him, but he seems pretty nice. He didn't give me too much of a hard time. He doesn't seem sold on the idea of you being here, though. Did you notice that?" Don asked in his deep, gravelly voice.

"Oh, yes, I noticed, Don. There's nothing subtle about Garold Limp. I'm afraid I've allowed myself to minimize how difficult he can be. For the last seven years I've only visited with his granddaughters in tow. He shows a very different side when I'm here with them. He's very patient and gentle then. And without them here as a distraction, I don't know what to expect. Plus, he's sick and he's a male, and we all know men are horrible patients!"

Don rolled his eyes and groaned at my male bashing. "What's his relationship like with your daughters?" Don asked.

Adoration was the only way to describe Dad's relationship with my girls. They were crazy about him and vice versa. It was impossible to ignore that he was much kinder to my children than to my sister's son and daughter. Giving him the benefit of the doubt, I decided part of the reason might be because he saw my children so seldom and hers so often. But I knew this was no excuse for his criticism and tough attitude toward my niece and nephew. More than once, I heard him speak to them with less than respect, and one incident in particular caused Dad and me not to speak to each other for many months.

"We had all gathered at my house—my parents, and my sister and her children. By this time my sister had divorced their father after a drunken episode where he fired a gun in their apartment. Little Derek, who was probably no more than five years old at the time, had been told several times not to climb on the huge ficus tree on our patio. Boys climb and that's what he continued to do. On his last attempt, he slipped and fell onto the concrete. Scraped up a little, he started to cry.

"My dad blew a gasket. He bent down and directed his tirade face to face to little Derek, and his words sent a chill down my whole body. I'd heard those harsh, judgmental words in that iniquitous tone of voice before. I half expected him to pull out his belt and use it. The memory was not a pleasant one."

"Other than not speaking later, how did the two of you handle that situation?" Don asked.

"Oh, like Limps, with no grace or tolerance. We went about three months without talking to each other, which made for some really awkward moments when I called home and he answered the phone. When we finally did speak again, the issue was just swept under the rug like so many other incidents. I still can't believe how bullheaded he is."

"How bullheaded *he* is?" Don said.

"Okay, I guess I'm a little bullheaded, too." We laughed and it reminded me that it was one of the great things about belonging to Alcoholics Anonymous. We learned to laugh at ourselves. It was an integral part of the recovery process.

"I'd better hit the sack since my flight is early tomorrow. The fire is almost gone anyway. Don't worry, Annie. This will all work out— one day at a time. Don't expect too much of them," Don whispered as he put his arm around me. We headed to the house where everything was dark except for a few fireflies scattered about and the patio light Mom had left on for us.

Chapter Nineteen

I came to realize long before adulthood that learning skills of diplomacy were not part of our family agenda. Mom perhaps wasn't aware of the concept of social etiquette, and Dad had no patience or tolerance for visceral platitudes.

As a young child, having company come to visit was a real treat because we just didn't get many visitors. It was not hard to tell that Dad was just fine with that. At the sight of a car coming up our driveway, he would start to pace and curse. He didn't want any damn company, as he called anyone he considered an intruder.

Dad said, "Good visitors are like good neighbors, they never show up at your front door. The less you see of them, the better."

I watched with confusion each time Dad morphed into Mr. Congeniality the minute the guests were *in* the house. And just as quickly, the minute good-bye passed over his lips, his words of contempt for the departed spewed from him like the steam from a pressure cooker that's preparing to blow.

"Some people don't have the common sense God granted a goose. Those damn people never know when to leave," he would complain before our visitors even got out of the driveway.

After company left, I always felt guilty, which was confusing because I hadn't invited them. Nonetheless, I remained quiet and baffled by his contiguous masks of hospitality and angry isolation. I longed for, and enjoyed, the company and it looked like Mom did, too.

On several occasions when a child was among our unwanted guests, I would be delighted to find that he or she had brought their own toys—a doll, a truck, a jump rope. Didn't seem to matter to me what size or shape, at least one of these toys would turn up missing when it came time for them to leave. I made sure of that by hiding it behind some towels in a hallway linen closet. Looking back, I believe part of me wanted the toy and part of me hoped the hidden toy would mean the child would have to come back one day to pick it up. Having visitors was such a treat. It made our family seem normal in some odd way.

After I'd pulled this stunt several times, Mom got wise to me. She found my hiding place and started looking there first when things went missing. I overheard her telling Dad one night after company left, "I think she hides those toys because she's so lonesome for the companionship of kids her age."

Dad's response, as always, was shot straight from the hip, quick draw, and to the point. "Bullshit. She gets that behavior from your shady side of the family. We know they're all liars and thieves. I just hope we don't have ourselves a thief in training."

I watched Mom after Dad spewed many of those hateful comments and I knew from her lack of response that, like myself, she hadn't found his words amusing. That's how she often handled his comments, particularly when they were cutting and sarcastic. She would stare at him for a few moments with small, dark eyes of frustration and then turn her diminutive frame and walk away, retreating to her cigarettes and television or just somewhere out of sight.

I always wondered if she cried after such incidents, but I was afraid to ask and often too scared to go look for her. They were moments of shame I carried with me into the next day, and the day after, and the day after that.

83

One night after overhearing his hateful words, somewhere deep inside me right in the pit of my stomach, I recalled a tiny spark of a fire. That blaze ignited, was stoked with anger, and grew just a little more intense each time I heard him wound Mom's spirit again.

Chapter Twenty

A few weeks after my arrival, Mom, Dad, and I began to settle into a routine. Maybe it would be more accurate to say that I started to assimilate myself into their routine, the one they had developed and lived for the last twenty-eight years of their marriage. We watched television, made trips to the grocery store, and organized doctor appointments on the phone.

A big treat for Mom and me became lunch or coffee at Babb's Restaurant. Babb's was a truck stop and a local favorite for semi drivers and farmers. Counter service was king here, and the waitresses' lingo included "honey, darling, good-looking, and sweetie pie." Dad said, "There is more sugar dripping from their lips than there is in the rhubarb strawberry pie they're known for!" Mom told me more than once that these gals were tough. Everyone knew better than to mess with them. There was no doubt they could sling mud as well as they could sling hash. I'd heard Dad say, "Those gals can butter your toast or slice off your breakfast sausage and they don't rightly care which one it is."

When Mom heard Dad say this, she leaned over and whispered to me, "What he really means is they know how to handle the men!"

Mom had gone off to Babb's this morning before I woke up. I found Dad in the kitchen slicing a tomato for his breakfast. I could tell when I said good morning that he was a little grouchy so I tried to tread quietly. The proverbial "walking on eggshells" routine was one I had perfected in childhood and it was still proving to be necessary. There were many days when Dad wasn't even friendly to me and this felt like it might be one of those miserable days. I tried to cut him some slack and remember he wasn't feeling well. But I had to admit, it still hurt. I nursed my wounds by reminding myself that Mom, at least, seemed to be appreciating my company and attempt to help.

Maybe my presence was providing Mom with a little escape from responsibility. After all, she had never embraced the role of being in charge. I wasn't sure if it was a role she chose not to take part in, or if Dad was her roadblock to any and every avenue of independence. He had never encouraged her to have friends. Verbally and mentally punished on the rare occasion that she chose to have lunch or coffee with one of her few buddies, there was always a price to pay afterward. Like a heckler in a crowd, Dad was relentless with his sarcastic, demeaning comments, and then the cold shoulder punishment would ensue for days. It appeared to be one of his favorite forms of mental terrorism. I could understand why Mom had seemingly turned her back on any friends. It just wasn't worth the punishment and ridicule.

When Mom returned from Babb's, she yelled to me from the garage, "Annie, come out here. You won't believe what I just heard. Jack Sayre had a heart attack and died."

Everyone has a best high school friend and Patty Sayre had been mine. I was shocked to hear that her father had died. Patty and I survived third and fourth grade together.

"That's awful. Have you heard anything about Patty all these years?" I asked.

"Nope. Not a word," Mom replied. "Remember Robert Shannon?"

I laughed at the memory. Patty and I had shared a forbidden friendship with Robert Shannon. He was a fuzzy-headed black boy in our third grade class that made us all laugh. He danced on top of his desk whenever the teacher left the room. He entertained us by doing all the things we were afraid to do. He was with us one summer when Patty and I spotted a hand grenade in a wooded area near us that we had named the Jungle. The Jungle was a fenced-in, overgrown lot behind a train station littered with abandoned steel tubes, old railroad cars, and other bits and pieces of the railroad industry. We'd worked hard to make a hole in the corner of the fence so we could sneak in, and because it was private property, it made it even more fun to explore.

Mom called the police when we told her about the hand grenade. We knew for sure we were going to be locked up. The police arrived and determined it was not a live grenade and was probably just a souvenir that had been discarded. We got dirty looks from the police officer and a scolding from our parents, but it sure livened up our summer.

Many days right after school, the three of us climbed on the coal that was piled ten or fifteen feet high near the railroad tracks. Robert doubled over with laughter when the black dust from the coal began to turn our white skin the same color as his.

At home, I found out quickly that my parents didn't think playing in the coal or playing with a black boy was funny, and I was pretty sure Patty heard the same rhetoric from her parents. I couldn't understand what all the fuss was about. After all we were just playing on the railroad tracks like Dad told us to do.

Patty was my confidante and my idol. Her family was Catholic. I'd never known a Catholic before. I thought she went to church an awful lot, though. I missed her on Sunday mornings. Many times I walked to the corner where her church was located and I sat on the curb waiting impatiently for the Sunday service to be over. I wondered what went on in there. From the outside, the stained-glass windows sparkled with colors as bright as I'd ever seen. I imagined what the building must look like inside. I felt alone and much less important than those inside, even though I didn't know most of them. I was envious that she and her family attended every Sunday.

Patty's family also belonged to the country club. I'd never heard of the place before meeting Patty. It was near the Girl's Club and I assumed it was for rich people and not for families like mine. I waited impatiently at home when Patty spent time at the country club. I heard her stories of swimming and barbeques. I dreamed of what it must look like there. I thought about what the people wore and what they talked about. Once again, I felt alone and less than those mysterious people that were part of this exclusive club.

Near the end of one summer, Patty's mom invited me to the club to swim with them. It was my first invitation. I could barely contain my excitement as I ran home to tell Mom and get my swimsuit. I was going to "the club."

When I returned with swimsuit in hand, I was met at the door by one of Patty's older sisters. She was the red-headed sister and the meanest of the three.

"What are you doing with the swimsuit?" she asked.

"Your mom invited me to the club with you guys," I said.

"What? You can't go the club. You're not a member. Your dad doesn't make enough money to be a member," she retorted in a snarky tone.

The rest of her words landed on my back, because I turned away from her glare and her nasty words, running as fast as I could. When I reached home, I stayed outside on our front porch and cried. I didn't want Mom to see me. How could I explain to her that we weren't good enough for the club? I couldn't face the embarrassment.

Later in the day, when Patty's mom found out what had happened, she called my mom and apologized and asked me again to join them. But for me, the idea was ruined. I was paralyzed with shame and pity for myself and my family. Despite repeated invitations that summer, I was too ashamed to ever go to the club.

By the end of the summer, I realized with sadness that my friendship with Patty had taken a fatal hit that day. I was never able to look at her the same after that. The crevice between what I believed to be her family and mine seemed too wide. Still stinging from the hurt and shame, I could see that I could never be a part of her life, so I closed the door on her world and on her. It was a scenario I would unconsciously recreate over and over again in the years to follow. Believing others determined my worth, coming face to face with unmet goals, and wrongly perceiving signs of disapproval from others, led me to abandoning people, places, and things that appeared to have turned against me.

Chapter Twenty One

Call it restlessness or a lack of self-understanding (over the years many psychologists identified it by many other names for me), but I was haunted by the nagging, although intellectually unfounded belief, that my parents were leading less than fulfilling lives. I hadn't figured out yet that judging other people's experiences by one's own expectations is dangerous territory. And though grossly misguided, my intentions were always sincere. I couldn't see the contradiction in wanting for them what I didn't really have—happiness and peace of mind.

After all, my glimpse of the big, wide world was well underway. Working as a flight attendant, followed by the privilege of marrying into wealth, had given me the opportunity to see a side of life I just knew my parents longed for, but were being cheated out of. I remember saying, "Mom, you've never been to a New York play. I just know you'd love it," or "Dad, wouldn't you like to visit the White House or the Capitol? Everyone should do it at least once,"

It did not occur to me when stacked up against a trip to the local Elks Club or a Friday night fish fry at the VFW, that any trip or sight I might plan for them would not measure up. I never once considered that mind reading might not be one of my better talents, or that their lives had turned out exactly as they had planned. I saw it as my mission to provide them with culture—to show them the finer things in their final quarter of the game of life. I concluded that their social life consisted of drinks a few nights a week in a local, seedy bar where many of the patrons were toothless, jobless, and drunk ninety percent of the time. I doubted there was a person in the joint who knew the difference between a cabernet and a chardonnay. My parents deserved better than this despite the fact that they didn't even drink wine.

In my heart, if not my head, I knew I could help make these good things happen for them. I was not aware of these misperceptions and how they had led me into rocky terrain as I arrived in Indiana with plans for enriching their lives.

As soon as I'd made the decision to go to Indiana, parent projects were put to paper. I compiled a list of tasks I planned to accomplish while nursing my parents back to health. Good health was important, but I also wanted to improve their lives. I felt like I owed it to them. After all, I was one of the few lucky ones from our family who had managed to escape the small town with small ideas.

I believed the steps to upgrade their existence would have to include fresh flowers in the house, an increased appreciation of music, fine dining, and an experiential appreciation for the luxuries of life. It did briefly occur to me that they had never mentioned a longing for any of these necessities, but I brushed the doubt aside by reminding myself that I had done more and seen more, and therefore I knew better.

My second night at home I announced I would be cooking dinner for them. Mom said, "Oh, honey, you don't have to do that. Dad and I usually just have something simple such as a bologna sandwich or some soup."

But I was insistent. "No, Mom, you're going to have some good meals from now on. I want to do that for you." It might have been my imagination, but I could have sworn I saw Dad raise his eyebrow as he lowered the newspaper just enough to throw a look in my direction.

"Well that's great, honey. I guess I wasn't aware you knew how to cook," Mom replied.

The truth was I didn't know how to cook. The first meal I cooked for them was not exactly gourmet or successful. It did, however, provide an opportunity for me to remember how unappreciative and vocal Dad could be when it came to mealtime.

Mom never once claimed to be a good cook. Her idea of a good meal was cottage cheese and frozen haddock, usually under- or overcooked, and smothered in ketchup. ??? Meals were a little hit-and-miss. Sometimes we did just have a bologna sandwich, and often we just rooted around the kitchen for snacks. Growing up it seemed perfectly normal to us. We didn't know what we didn't know—that other mothers cooked every day, and families sat down and ate together every day.

Occasionally, Mom got inspired to up her cooking repertoire. We suspected her inspiration was borne of boredom or a shortage of bologna at the market. She would timidly venture outside the box of her mediocre skills and try a new recipe or creation she'd heard about on television. Each time, without fail, and often before the meal was even served, Dad would knock the proverbial wind out of her sails with his nasty comments about her planned meal. She'd had the rug pulled out from under her so many times that she should have been black and blue. If the meal wasn't to his liking, the insults would fly. I vividly remember watching him shove his plate away, stand up, and stomp away from the table. In these moments, my sister and I tried to compensate for his anger with words of encouragement to Mom. We spoke in small, quiet voices so he couldn't hear. We were embarrassed and scared when, on rare occasions, Mom's humiliation turned into anger and defiance.

"What a miserable person he is! I'll be damned if I cook for him again" she would yell. More than once we saw her drop his plate, food and all, into the sink and walk away.

Meanwhile, he was off sulking somewhere and would later
sneak back into the kitchen for a bologna sandwich with mayo and
mustard—and hold the apology, please.

Ah, yes. Here I was twenty-five years later and starting to
remember how much fun mealtimes were. In lieu of home cooking,
I brilliantly planned a lunch outing for the whole family to Olive
Garden. I knew they very seldom ate out. Dad was quick to point out
that he didn't care for eating out and was a very unwilling participant
as we waited for our table. He stood in the corner with feet planted
like a mule who wasn't moving anywhere, his hands in the pockets of
his tan jacket and looking like someone who had been taken hostage
by three obnoxious, chattering females.

Once seated, our young, timid waitress blushed easily as
Dad teased and questioned her. "I can't seem to find the good ol'
sandwiches on this menu. Could you point them out?" Dad asked.
She was forced to deliver the bad news—there were no sandwiches
on the menu.

Julie tried to help him make a selection, but to no avail. Dad
quickly gave up on what he considered all the menu's fancy choices
and just ordered a beer. We cowered in embarrassment truly not
knowing what to do with him. In desperation, we finally ordered
a simple ravioli dish for him. We knew the choice didn't make any
difference, because no entree was going to escape his condemnation.
In the end, of course, Dad proved us right.

I ate with a nervous stomach and a huge desire for not a glass,
but a barrel of red wine to calm the anticipation of never hearing the
end of this story about the miserable Italians who didn't know how to
cook or run a restaurant. Mom and Julie had the wine *I* needed. I had
a diet soda.

On our way out, Mom grabbed a toothpick as she always did.
At the door, Dad grabbed one of the mints near the register like

a hungry animal deprived of food. As he zipped up his jacket, he mumbled under his breath, "Next time, leave me at home and I'll have a bologna sandwich."

Giving them the experience of dining out. I marked that one off my list of projects.

The next item on my list of projects was fresh flowers. Bringing home a bouquet, regardless of how small and inexpensive it was, always made me feel good about myself and I hoped it would do the same for them. I brought the first bouquet home and proudly placed it on the kitchen table. I had barely finished arranging it when Dad walked through the room and referred to them as weeds.

"Now why in God's name would you waste your money on those weeds?" he asked.

Fresh flowers. I could mark those off my list as well.

Chapter Twenty Two

Dad's vacation from chemo treatments ended. Today would be his first day back at the chemo suite as the nurses called it. His voice and manner were subdued as he commented on the coming rain that he could see off in the distance. It was as if overnight he had aged twenty years and his spirit had taken a dive into the deep.

"Dad, what time do you want to leave for your doctor appointment?" I asked.

"Ask your mom, Annie. I've lost track."

Between his and Mom's schedule, we had some medical obligation almost every day. We were either making appointments on the phone, going to appointments, or picking up medications at the pharmacy. It was nonstop. I wondered how they could have handled it all if I wasn't there to help. My sister worked full-time so she wouldn't have been able to do it.

Today was Dad's turn at the doctor's office. Mom and I shared his nervousness even though we tried not to show it. Today's topic with the doctor would be treatment options. When I thought of the word "options," I had always pictured add ons, or perks, like when you buy a car or get stock issued from your employer. Good stuff. Bad stuff. Choices between further radiation or chemotherapy just didn't seem like they should be part of an option package, but this time I knew they were going to be.

Dad was taken back to a room to meet with the doctor while Mom and I filled out paperwork in the lobby. I was starting to understand the reason there were aquariums in many of the doctors' offices we visited. The fish swam tranquilly along like they had no worries. If I watched them long enough, I could almost forget the reason we were here.

Not long after Dad had been taken to the back, a very pleasant and smiling nurse lead us to an examining room where we found him, still in his hospital gown, sitting on the edge of the examining table. There were anatomy charts hanging all over the walls and that hideous smell of disinfectant that permeates medical facilities. As soon as I caught a glimpse of my dad in the paper gown, I was torn between laughing and crying. But the laughter won out as soon as he began to complain about icicles forming on his backside.

"Why the hell do these open in the back?" Dad asked.

"It's an age-old question, Dad. I remember when Katie was in the hospital. Do you guys remember? She was only four, I think. She had a febrile seizure and they put her in the hospital for a week. She was so cute in her hospital gown with her little butt cheeks hanging out. Of course I took pictures of her, and had the opportunity to embarrass her several times by showing the images to some of her friends. I could take some photos of your butt cheeks, Grandpa."

"I don't think so," Dad said as he tugged on his gown.

Before the doctor came into the room, I asked, "What did the doctor have to say, Dad?" I feared the answer as I always did after his doctor appointments.

With concerted awkwardness, Dad stood and began to untie his gown and lower it to his waist as he said to us, "Well, guys, look at this." He pointed to his chest.

His chest area had been branded with a permanent black marker indicating the target area that would be blasted with radiation. He showed it off like a badge of honor or a newly acquired tattoo. The marks extended from one shoulder blade all the way across his collarbone to the other side and down the middle of his ribcage to just above his navel. It was a shocking and ghastly sight. I had never seen a marker used on a human body like that, and I had never noticed the few gray curly hairs on Dad's chest.

I turned away, holding back the anger and the tears, and thinking markers should be used for labeling boxes and storage bins for Christmas decorations, not for human body parts fallen prey to cancer. But there were the markings pinpointing the area of disease on his pale emaciated breastbone. I hated that permanent marker smell and I abhorred the disease underneath it.

"The radiation doesn't start until next week, but today I'm going in for another round of chemo. Fun. Fun. You guys don't need to stay. Come back and get me later," Dad said.

Just then the surgeon came into the room. He was short and serious looking. I remember thinking he had no expression on his face. I didn't know him, but I hated him instantly. He didn't even bother to acknowledge Mom and me except to throw us a look like we were some unwanted loiterers in a prohibited area. He proceeded to explain to Dad that the results of radiating in this area could make his throat raw and vulnerable to infection, and at some point, his ability to swallow might be compromised.

I watched Dad's face as the doctor spoke and drew a diagram of Dad's abdomen on a dry erase board. Dad's face looked just like the doctor's—expressionless. He looked like he'd been hypnotized. His eyes were glazed over and he was as still as a statue. I wondered if he was even hearing what the doctor was saying.

We waited until we were able to walk Dad back into the infusion area. It was a bright room painted yellow with lots of windows. I thought of the studies I'd read about the effects certain colors have on our moods. Red for energy. Blue for calmness. Maybe yellow was supposed to help one forget they had cancer. It was obvious they had made an effort to take some of the clinical, medical feel out of the space. It actually smelled pleasant, too.

Around the room, reclining chairs were positioned about every ten feet. Each station, as the nurses called them, had blankets, pillows, and an assortment of magazines spread out on what looked like a hospital's version of TV tray tables. Most of the chairs were empty today except for a young, red-headed girl who had her head buried in a video game, and an elderly man whose snoring periodically pierced the otherwise hushed atmosphere.

Dad had already been fitted with a medical port, so hooking him up was quick and effortless. I'd actually overheard a conversation between my parents discussing their ports. Mom was hesitant to have hers removed even though she wasn't scheduled for any more treatment. Now that Dad had one, she wanted to keep hers, too. I might have thought they were crazy except I had known that feeling before, but as a child. Once when my sister fell out of a tree and broke her arm, I longed for a cast just like hers. I thought it was so cool. So I kind of understood that my parents were regressing into adolescence.

I stared at the bag attached to Dad's IV. The liquid was clear and looked so harmless and ordinary, but I knew the look was deceiving. I had done enough research to know the power and the side effects of the poison that was slowing dripping into his bloodstream.

After the completion of his chemotherapy, radiation began. Each day of treatment was like a reoccurring nightmare. On the way home, he was weaker, nauseous, and more depressed. Arriving home from the appointments, he disappeared into his bedroom where he and Hooper would remain for most of the day. Mom and I usually spent the afternoon hours watching soap operas. There was very little conversation on treatment days. We couldn't find any words to say, and we wouldn't have had the emotional strength to say them anyway.

Chapter Twenty Three

Autumn was arriving quickly in the Crossroads of America, but phone calls from my girls let me know it was still very hot in Florida.

"Mom, Dad won't let us buy our pumpkins yet," Chelsea moaned over the phone one afternoon. "He said it's too early."

"I want my own pumpkin this year. Can I, Mom?" Katie asked when she finally got the receiver away from her sister.

Halloween, one of my favorite holidays, was right around the corner and there was no missing its arrival with pumpkins, scarecrows, and black and orange decorations everywhere. Growing up in the Midwest, we bought our pumpkins weeks ahead, carved them, placed them outside, and never missed a night of lighting the candles once it was dark. I understood my girls' frustration and their dad's reasoning for waiting to buy their pumpkins, though. In Florida's heat and humidity, the pumpkin didn't have a chance of survival, even if you waited until the night before to carve it. I tried this explanation on the phone with the girls, but they were not convinced or consoled.

Maybe people in Indiana had more respect for Halloween or produce, in general, because in Florida if your pumpkin didn't rot before Halloween night, chances were good you'd find it in a pile in the middle of the street where some mean neighbor kid had hurled it.

I handed the phone to Dad so he could talk to the girls. I listened as he teased them and asked them about school. It was so good to hear him laugh. Mom and I had noticed he was having a spurt of energy the last few days and his spirits were much more positive as well. He was taking advantage of the energy, spending his time doing some of his favorites things—working in the yard, tinkering in the barn, and bantering about anything and everything with anyone who would listen or participate. He was also as aggravating as usual, but that was a good sign, and we accepted it because we were so grateful for any signs of improvement.

My girls were flying in to spend a couple of days with us. I missed them beyond words. There hadn't been a day since I'd left them that I didn't question whether I was doing the right thing leaving them behind. But now I was here and all I could do was pray for the.

We talked on the phone at least once a day. Several times I got my feelings hurt when their attention was diverted away from our conversation to something happening on their end of the wire. I complained and they apologized, but many times these conversations ended abruptly as they engaged in the activity and the people that were in the room with them. I was left holding the receiver, silence on the other end, and remembered how my own mother had once complained to me about how I often hung up on her so abruptly. She had said one minute we would be discussing something and the next I would say, "Gotta go, Mom," and click, I was gone. Now I was beginning to understand how she felt when she heard that click. Watching my daughters was often like looking into a mirror. Frightening and funny at the same time.

I was trying to keep current on the girls' school activities and anything else that was going on. When I asked about their Halloween costumes, they described in vivid detail the costumes they were bringing with them on the plane. I smiled as I remembered many years previously when they were younger, how much I enjoyed making their costumes. One year Chelsea was a traffic light fashioned out of a cardboard box with holes cut out and colored paper inserted for the red, yellow, and green lights. She was adorable in it. The following year, Dalmatians were popular and both girls were admired at school for their matching white with black spots outfits, including dog ears and red dog collars. I enjoyed making them almost as much as I enjoyed others admiring the results. I was pretty sure that when I was young, my costumes had been put together with whatever was available around the house. Creating a costume was a rare chance Mom had to be creative. Besides, it was usually cold on Halloween and a winter coat ended up covering up the majority of whatever we were wearing. And we didn't trick or treat on just one night or in one neighborhood. Maybe because we lived in a rural area, but for three or four nights in a row we loaded up in the car and headed out to a nearby neighborhood where we knocked on doors and carried our loot home with glee.

After each phone conversation, I sensed the girls wanted to ask me when I was coming home, but somehow they intuitively knew the question would really be asking when, and if, Grandpa was going to get better. I could hear the conflict in their voices. I was finding it difficult to be positive and hopeful about Dad's condition while maintaining some semblance of truth with them.

The girls often ended our phone conversations with, "Tell Grandma and Grampy we love them, and we love you, too, Mommy. We can't wait for our visit! See you when you pick us up at the airport."

Thinking of the girls' flight reminded me of the times I used to call my mom and dad after stepping off an airplane and on my way to a layover with the rest of my crew. Those long ago conversations were like a travelogue of where I was and what it looked like.

"Hi, Mom! Guess where I am?" I would say as I wheeled my suitcase into a hotel room.

"Where are you, hon?" Mom would ask.

"I'm looking out the window of the Monte Carlo Hotel in Las Vegas," I replied as I looked down at all the lights below. "The view here is awesome. I wish you could see it. Boy, do I love layovers, especially in cities like this one."

"Oh, you lucky dog!" Mom exclaimed. I could hear the excitement in her voice as she relayed the info to my dad. "Your dad said to play some blackjack for him. How long are you there? Do you have a nice crew?"

My folks never quite got over the excitement of my airline job, and I never got tired of the gratitude I had for being able to give them the opportunity to fly on my airline passes. I didn't know it at the time, but found out many years later, that Mom had kept a copy of every pass she and Dad ever used. On each pass she had written trip details such as "Had a great time," "Got bumped in Atlanta," "Bad weather during the flight," and "Got to see the grandchildren again."

I could picture one autumn when my parents and I took a trip to San Francisco. It was a cool and crisp outside. The cable cars, winding streets, and other activity—we relished it all before retiring that evening to a room where we could hear the waves crashing onto the beach. Mom said it was heaven. Dad couldn't get over the enormous amount of wealth the locals had. It was the same observation he made in any new place. He would say, "My God. How do these people make all their money?"

I took his comment as a sign of longing for riches. I felt sorry for him. The man had worked so hard all his life and, by wealth standards, had so little to show for it. What I didn't know was that when he returned home, the other Garold showed up. His comment to his buddies was, "That San Francisco is beautiful, but I wouldn't live there for any amount of money. Too noisy, too busy. I like it out here in the country."

His marveling at the sights was just a tourist's observation, not a personal longing. But from my perspective of discontent and restlessness, I mistook his comments to be a desire to be someone else, and to be somewhere else. I was seeing him through *my* loneliness.

Chapter Twenty Four

Sunday afternoon had brought us an unusual warm spell and Dad was the making the most of it by washing his truck and Mom's car. Dad had always been a little compulsive about his washing and waxing routine. He even gave his riding lawnmower the same pampering. As kids we teased him about it. Now as an adult, I realized he was most relaxed when he was doing mundane activities like cutting the grass, trimming the shrubs, or driving into town to pick up the newspaper. These were the things that made him happy.

I'd never had any doubt that the people and life here were much simpler and more wholesome than they were in Florida. My parents still left the keys in their vehicles. It hadn't been that many years ago when they still left them in the ignition. Now they at least put them on the floor or under the floor mat. I could imagine the results of this practice in Florida. No car in no time.

In many ways, this area was behind the times in technology and culture, but they were way ahead in matters of the heart. I had to admit I missed the sense of honesty that most people in the area seemed to instinctively have. With Dad being the exception, there was a civility that I hadn't experienced in a long time.

On rare peaceful and healthy days, I was lulled into forgetting how cruel Dad could be. It had been a long time since I'd seen him in action on a regular basis. However, I hadn't forgotten he had never been big on personal freedom of any kind for anyone. I laughed when I remembered this, realizing I had some of that tendency as well.

One afternoon, Dad was napping and Mom and I sat quietly at the kitchen table. I often found myself asking her questions about the past because my memory was less than keen. Sometimes she seemed a little put off by this, so I broached a topic a little gingerly as I asked, "Do you remember what Dad used to do to the car tires when Julie and I were little and we lived out by Sugar Creek?"

She looked at me with a blank stare for a moment, and then broke into a smile and said, "Oh yeah. That bastard used to keep track of when we moved the car. I haven't thought of that in years."

We laughed and drank our coffee as we recounted the details together.

Along with learning our ABCs and the capitals of the states, my sister and I also learned to recognize the look on Mom's face when we were going to pull one. That's what she called it when we disobeyed Dad's rules. Whatever we were about to do, it was usually exciting and meant a trip to town or some extra money for us.

We didn't get to go many places. Dad didn't allow us to. I never heard him acknowledge it, but even to a small child I could tell he kept Mom on a very short leash. I never knew where he was afraid she would go, but the car was not to be moved without his permission, not even for a simple trip to the store or just to run an errand. We were not to move the car. Because we lived out in the country, there wasn't much to do. And Mom got bored easily. Occasionally, she got what we came to recognize as "the look" and that meant a little jaunt into town, regardless of the consequences that might ensue.

After one short trip, Dad came home asking where we had been. Mom thought this was odd since she hadn't mentioned going anywhere. It happened several times after that as well. We were puzzled. How did he know? We didn't dare ask as each time he expressed his disapproval with a louder angst than the time before. Mom would get the third degree and the accompanying insults.

But sooner or later, Mom's bruised feelings would heal, and the travel bug would strike her again. One day as we prepared to escape our home confinement, we discovered Dad's covert tactics. He was marking one of the tires with chalk so he could tell if the car had been moved. Mom winked at us and said, "No problem. We know how to play that game!"

So we erased his chalk mark and off to town we went. When we returned from our drive, we took great care to place the chalk mark right where it had been before we moved the car. This worked for a while. Then, several trips later, Dad must have figured out we were moving the car again and as usual, he was one step and four wheels ahead of us. This time he caught us by marking the location of the stem on one of the tires. We were busted again. We tried sneaking around a couple of times after that. Mom would drive back and forth in the driveway until I gave her the signal that the tire stem was in the right spot. But this turned out to be an almost impossible operation.

Home became our cage, and periodically, at his discretion, the chalk-carrying zookeeper would allow us out to roam a little.

Mom sat her coffee cup down on the counter as she said, "That was such a long time ago. We finally gave up on trips to town, didn't we, honey?"

I nodded my head in agreement as I looked out the kitchen window and noticed the rain had snuck up on us while we were reminiscing. It was a steady stream, but soft and quiet, just like my voice as I answered, "Yes, I guess we did give up, Mom."

I didn't say it out loud, but I thought that we'd given up on a lot of things during those years.

Chapter Twenty Five

It was the first time I'd slept in a twin bed in years. And just like most childhood icons you recall being larger than life, my bed seemed much smaller than I remembered. The buildings looked smaller, and our little town seemed tinier even though it now had two traffic lights instead of one. Even the creek that ran through the park looked as if it had shrunk in size.

I was enjoying waking up in the morning to the cool temperatures of a winter fast approaching. The South American wild parrots we had in Fort Lauderdale were beautiful to look at, but were so noisy they could drown out just about anything with their high-pitched screeching. Here in the country we had the sweet sounds of indigenous birds singing their morning songs. I couldn't get over how fresh the air smelled.

The aroma of coffee drew me to the kitchen this morning. As I walked down the hallway, I saw Dad standing and looking out the front door. The screen door hadn't been replaced yet with the storm door, but soon would be as the weather deteriorated. It wasn't unusual for Mom to have all the blinds and doors open because she loved it bright inside. She said a dark house made her depressed and reminded her of her childhood.

The light from the door was shining through the few wiry hairs still left on the top of Dad's head. He didn't stir, but must have heard me come up behind him as he said, "Remember the day we put up the flagpole, Annie? You helped me with it."

I stepped closer to the door and looked out where Dad's flagpole rose nearly thirty feet in the air near the middle of the yard. "Oh, I remember. I couldn't hold on to the pole and you nearly killed me when we tried to lift it up and put it into the ground!"

Dad laughed and said, "It's held up pretty good after all these years. Your old papa's pretty good at things like that, huh?"

"Yes, you are Dad. I don't think there's another one like it around here."

"Your mom and I have gone through a lot of flags all these years." His voice trailed off but his gaze toward the yard remained constant.

I don't think any of us ever questioned Dad's patriotism. It was a quiet loyalty, unlike most of his beliefs, but it hadn't surprised any of us when he decided to put up the flagpole.

As I walked on into the kitchen I watched him continue gazing out the door. I wondered what he was thinking about, just like I wondered why we hadn't heard him ranting and raving about the recent terrorist attacks. It was so unlike him. I'd never seen him this quiet and reflective. The change I saw in him hurt and scared me.

Each morning before I encountered Dad, and unconsciously evaluated his deteriorating condition, I vowed to myself to start with a new energy and a renewed determination to make a difference, and to make the situation here better. I wasn't sure how, but I was going to do it.

Don was still calling me from Fort Lauderdale every day or so just to check in. I knew he was worried about my sobriety.

"Don't let your dad get to you, Annie. Remember to take care of yourself, and don't pick up a drink. One day at a time. Are you going to enough meetings?" he always asked right before we hung up the phone.

I realized I had no choice about going to meetings. They were my lifeline and also served as a temporary escape from reality. Sitting among strangers in locations I'd never been to before, gave me the chance to forget about the limbo I found myself stuck in.

Here, just like in Florida, twelve step meetings, and the sites of the meeting rooms, guaranteed a hard to find location and assorted cast of characters. Being constantly lost, geographically and many other ways, I could always find the meeting if I could get within a few blocks of it. There on a sidewalk or side porch would be a group of fairly normal-looking people gathered in a cloud of cigarette smoke and sucking down coffee from white styrofoam cups. And true to the miracle of the twelve step programs, upon arriving I always felt like I was home.

My parents seemed to respect my sobriety, although I'm sure they didn't understand it. I knew they were relieved, and even proud of me, for this accomplishment. But I also sensed their veneration about this mysterious recovery concept. They were intrigued by the number of meetings I attended, and stunned by some of the stories I brought home.

Not long after my arrival in Indiana, I found a Tuesday evening meeting in a small town not far from my parents' home. The meeting was scheduled for 7:00 p.m. and, always prepared to get lost, I arrived thirty minutes early as I usually did. The street address took me to a tiny wooden house that looked like it hadn't been painted or cared for since the horse and buggy era. It didn't surprise me that no one had arrived yet. It was a common character defect among alcoholics and addicts to always be tardy. Ten or fifteen minutes passed and finally a man showed up and expressed his concern that the door hadn't been opened yet. After a brief phone call, he apologetically explained to me that the only guy with a key to the place had been arrested overnight and was in jail.

Meeting canceled. Mom and Dad loved that story.

The following week, I tried the same meeting again. The door was unlocked this time. By 7:10 p.m., six men and I were in attendance. We were all so different from such diverse walks of life, and yet, as was always true, we shared a common bond. Our stories varied, but alcohol had treated us all the same. Once again, even here among strangers and some scary looking ones at that, I felt at home.

It was not until the meeting's end and we started to depart that I noticed every man in the room wore a monitoring bracelet on his ankle. I got in my car, locked the doors quickly, and made the decision to find some other Tuesday meeting. Mom and Dad listened to me with jaws dropped as I described the ankle jewelry on the other attendees.

Dad laughed and said, "Damn, Annie. Don't you think you could find better company than that at some bar?"

I understood what he was saying, but there would be no better company for me at any bar. I knew that for sure.

Dad walked away mumbling, "The higher the monkey climbs, the more of his ass you see." I had no idea what that meant.

I assured Don that I was attending meetings regularly. Each time I heard his voice, I became a little more appreciative of his friendship. Perhaps that's why I spared him from hearing many of the stories of the drunken brawls I'd seen as a kid. There were a lot of those memories coming up that hadn't surfaced in a long time. I assumed the familiar surroundings were giving them new life, and it was very discomforting.

Chapter Twenty Six

Most school children can't wait for the school year to end, and my girls were no exception. But when I was young, I couldn't wait for the school year to start. The smell of new textbooks, and at least one new dress to wear the first day of school, gave me a thrill unlike any other, except maybe Christmas morning.

A new dress didn't necessarily mean right from a department store. Often it meant new just to me because it was from our favorite store—Goodwill. Mom taught both my sister and me the joy of secondhand shopping. I truly wasn't aware that all families didn't shop there. Rummaging through the heaps of clothing and shoes, we always succeeded in coming home with a bagful of goodies. It was fun.

I loved homework. My room, which much to my parents' chagrin I painted a deep blue color, was my refuge and where I headed the minute I got off the school bus. The ride was a source of excitement, as well as fear, for me and something I looked forward to. However, catching the bus filled me with anxiety. If you weren't standing at the road when the bus arrived, the driver would honk twice and then pull away without you. This didn't happen to me often, but the mere chance that it might happen haunted me like a reoccurring nightmare.

I recalled one morning where I made it to the road on time but so did a new puppy we had just brought home. No more than a couple of months old, he trotted his fat little body down the driveway with Mom chasing after him. He followed me right onto the bus and, while trying to catch him, I fell down in the aisle and ripped both arms out of my winter coat. Then as if the humiliation couldn't get any worse, Mom arrived at the bus door in her pajamas where the bus driver handed over the squirming puppy. My bus phobia tripled. My phobias extended to rules as well—anyone's rules, and especially Dad's. Even the yellow lines on the school bus windows gave me anxiety. The lines were there to show how far down the window could safely be lowered. No matter how hot it was, I wouldn't have dared try to lower the window for fear I would go below the line.

In high school I gave the same bus driver another good laugh. Once I started to drive, my chariot was an old Chevy Nova. It had a mind of its own and only ran when it wanted to, and often stalled at traffic lights. In order to keep the engine from dying, it was necessary to put the car in neutral and keep my foot on the brake and accelerator at the same time. When I explained this problem to Dad, his response was, "You've got to be kidding. Sounds like driver error to me. I've never had a problem with that car. Maybe someone needs to go back to driver's education class."

One morning on the drive to school, I noticed the bus I usually rode on was behind me. The bus driver, who had grown up with my dad and served in the Navy with him, waved to me. I felt proud to be driving, but embarrassed as well. As an onset of nerves welled up in me, the light turned green and I mistakenly moved the gear shift from neutral to reverse instead of drive, and simultaneously stepped on the gas. The next sound I heard was my bumper hitting the bumper of the school bus. I knew it was a sound I wouldn't soon forget. I didn't dare look in the rearview mirror. I put the car in drive and took off through the intersection. I arrived at school nauseous and shaking, and praying the news of this morning's event never reached my father's ears.

But in a small town there are few secrets. Dad heard about me versus the bus just a few days later. He said, "Are you sure you should

be driving a car? Maybe we'd better go back to riding the school bus."
I didn't respond, but there was no way I was ever facing that bus
driver again! I'd walk to school before I'd step onto his bus.

Chapter Twenty Seven

Dad was granted a week's leave from chemotherapy. It was a celebration. His spirits were lifted, and he emerged from his bathroom on Friday night with his poo poo' powder on as he called his aftershave. Mom and I glanced over at each other. We knew what this meant—a little night out at Whit's Inn, their favorite watering hole. It had been a good while since Dad had felt good enough to go out. I decided to tag along.

Each state has its own local oddities and ours was no different. Florida has their iguanas, wet T-shirt contests, and conch fritters. Indiana has prize-winning bell pepper crops, which we call mangoes, an insatiable pride for basketball, and hog fries. Pretzels and peanuts for bar appetizers seemed pretty mundane compared to our local fare. We dressed up the name to be Hog Fries, but we all knew they were really pig testicles! And every bar owner knew they could increase your business twofold. Chicken wing night would always guarantee a good crowd, and pizza night brought out a lot of locals, but Hog Fry night meant you'd better get there early and never give up your seat if you were lucky enough to even get one.

Smoke-filled and poorly lit, Whit's Inn generously welcomed Mom and Dad with hugs, handshakes, and shouts of "Good to see you guys. It's been awhile." It was wonderful to see Dad smiling and enjoying himself. Watching him joke around with his buddies, I noticed how much his physical appearance had changed. Here in the space he loved, he looked almost like his former self, pre-cancer. Dad had a few beers and I watched as his energy and interest waned pretty quickly. I thought of all the nights they had left this place totally intoxicated. Dad said it was one of the advantages of living in a small town. The local police have a tendency to ignore drunk drivers if it might be detrimental to local businesses.

Yes, good for commerce, but not so good for vehicular fatalities, I thought.

Mom and Dad let me know they were ready to head home. I noticed Dad hadn't even finished his last beer. Never had I ever seen him leave any beer behind. This was undoubtedly a sign of his illness. He eased off the bar stool and struggled to navigate as so many people tried to say goodbye to him and Mom. As we left the bar, I was especially grateful for my sobriety this evening. Tonight my parents had a designated driver like they should have had all those nights before.

It was only since I'd sobered up that I realized how many events of our lives were centered around alcohol. As far back as I could remember, beer had always been a staple in our house. Had my grade school teachers asked me to name the four food groups, chances are I would have included beer as one of them.

If our plans included a picnic, it was Mom's fried chicken, buttered white bread, and a six-pack of brew. If we took a car ride, which we did quite often, a cooler of beer went along. Drive-in movies found my sister and I in pajamas, and the car stocked with beer and a 'pee can' for Dad so nature's call didn't mean a trip to the concession stand restroom. Occasionally, Mom and Dad had a few people over to the house to play card games. Sounds of raucous laughter and clouds of cigarette smoke wafted from the kitchen table. On these nights, I went to sleep in spite of the continuous popping sounds of long neck beer bottles being opened. The inside of my eyelids burned from the smoke. The older I got the more I realized I was growing up in a smoky haze.

Dad had transformed an old, white refrigerator in the garage into a pony keg station where the hose from the keg came right outside the body of the frig. We might be out of milk, but never out of beer, except maybe on Sunday.

Ours was a blue law county, meaning it was against the law to sell any liquor on Sundays. A day with no beer? No way. Dad would load us up in the car and after a short drive we'd end up in an alley where he knocked on a dirty door on the backside of an old building. He was always carrying two six-packs of beer when he returned. His bootlegger was the title he gave to the elderly black woman who answered the door. Later I found out her name was Mabel. She owned a bar called the Tanyika Inn. It was in the seedy part of town right behind the alley where Dad scored his brew. On one trip, Mabel actually waved to my sister and me as we waited in the car. A trip to Mabel's became pretty mundane to us, no more unusual than going to the store for a loaf of bread. This store just looked a lot different. I wondered if other families made this kind of Sunday afternoon outing.

Dad's drunks were pretty routine as well. The only show worse than his intoxicated state was his hangover. As soon as his bloodshot eyes opened the morning after his outing, his remorse was quickly swallowed up with anger and self-hate. His hangover became your hangover. His bad mood became your bad mood, whether you wanted it or not.

Sometimes on hungover mornings, I could hear Mom on the phone with Dad's boss. She would be explaining that Dad was sick and would not be coming in. I remember thinking it was sad Mom had to lie for him. Other times when he did get up, the cold silence between he and Mom would spread a chill over the whole house. Worse yet was the sound of his gravelly voice when he finally did decide to speak. His orders were spat out and they sliced through the silence. His toxic words were laden with humiliation and hate for anyone within hearing distance.

"Who the hell turned the heat up so high? And what is your mother burning this morning? That smell is awful. Get that blue shit off your eyes. You're not going to school looking like that! I don't suppose anyone fed the dog yet. Of course not! What are you looking at? Better hope your face doesn't freeze that way." As usual, he was shooting from the hip and his gun was fully loaded.

In an effort to avert his wrath, we moved through our morning routine with very little talk and absolutely no commotion. It was as if we were trying to breathe without breathing. We watched as he laced up his clodhopper work boots and stomped out of the house. Our collective sighs were audible. The drunken sailor had departed his ship, leaving behind his crew shaken, scarred, and worrying about the next battle.

Chapter Twenty Eight

It had been a long drive to Indiana but I hadn't told Don all the stories I remembered. One in particular had happened when I was still in middle school. I'd never told anyone about the butcher knife.

It was early evening and my sister and I were sprawled out on the living room floor watching our last few minutes of television before we would be reminded of bedtime. Mom was washing the dishes in the kitchen. She crossed the kitchen to answer the phone, barefoot and wearing her favorite old nightgown. She had just hung up the phone as I watched her wedge a long butcher knife into the frame of the doorway that connected our kitchen to the garage.

My sister and I glanced over at each other. We had seen her do this before. It was an ominous signal that Dad was drinking the hard stuff, as mom called it. It also meant he would arrive home as a force not to be reckoned with. The knife would prevent him from opening the door when he came home drunk and looking for a fight.

Mom tried to explain to us, "Dad isn't bad when he's just drinking beer, but that hard liquor makes him mean." Soon after her explanation, my sister and I were sent to our rooms. There was a brief lull of silence ,and then we heard Dad's car in the driveway. Even brick walls couldn't prevent us from hearing the uproar that exploded.

Of course Mom's knife turned out to be only a temporary solution. It wasn't the first time the frame of the door had to be replaced. Once inside the house, Dad jockeyed back and forth from a raging drunk into a pleading husband, and right back into the drunk over and over again.

The child in me cried and hovered in fright behind my bedroom door while the adult in me rose up and wanted to protect my Mom and my sister from this monster who earlier in the day had been my dad.

I was gratefully jarred back to the present by my phone's ring. It was Don, who had no way of knowing he had just rescued me from my past.

"Just checking in on you. Everything peaceful there?" he asked.

"We're doing okay, Don. I'm just working on keeping in the present moment."

I thought about sharing the story with him, but in the end decided against it. It was just too painful to repeat out loud. Besides, dwelling in the past made me very thirsty. I thought it better to listen to his stories of sobriety and how to keep it.

Chapter Twenty Nine

With my dad still on reprieve from chemo treatments, my schedule was clear for the next few days. Curiosity and a little boredom led me to driving around to places I hadn't seen in years—old grade school buildings, the skating rink, the Dairy Queen. I was trying to conjure up good childhood memories in hopes that the bad memories would recede. I was also trying to avoid the task of organizing my belongings that I had dumped in Dad's barn. I had made a real mess out of his usually organized space.

In each place we lived over the years, Dad always carved out a space for his tools and a wooden workbench. It seemed to my sister and me that Dad could build or fix just about anything. He could do the electric and plumbing, and he had even built a couple of homes, including this one. In this house, as he did in every one of our houses, he had erected his workspace in the back of the small red barn that sat on the edge of the property—the same space I had turned into a storage facility with all my belongings. He hadn't commented on the mess yet, but I knew it was coming sooner or later.

It was early morning. The country air smelled fresh and the quiet made me feel peaceful. I wandered out to the barn. It was a museum of dad things—old license plates, garden tools, scrap wood, and lawnmower parts. It all looked randomly placed, but Dad knew where every single item was hanging or tucked away. He labeled everything. If you needed something repaired or boxed to ship, Dad could get it done no matter the size or shape.

"Oh, my God. How are you going to get that home?" Mom exclaimed many times over the years as I arrived home from a shopping trip with items like an antique piano stool I had found at a consignment store. Dad usually couldn't resist commenting on the item's worthlessness, and chastised me for spending money. But I knew despite his attitude, he remained our in-house master box maker. There were mumbles and complaints the whole time he worked on it, but the final product would be a container just the right size and suitable for carry on, or checked, baggage depending on the object's size. He never let me down in this area.

All of the barn's storage area was in the front, and Dad's work area was toward the back where the old white Frigidaire (the same one that had once been transformed into the beer keg) was still working and stood proudly against the passage of time. Nowadays, fruit and vegetables from the garden, and beer and plant seeds, were usually its only occupants.

The barn looked just as it had since I was young. Above his workbench, Dad had mounted a large, brown pegboard with a hook to hold each of his tools. To make the process even tidier, he had drawn an outline around each tool with a black marker, indicating where it had been hanging previously. Each tool had a home, and after use, was always returned to its proper address. His work area always fascinated me. The sweet smell of oil, cut wood, and tobacco always lingered there. I drew some kind of comfort from the odors, almost like I was sneaking a peek at an intimate side of him that I didn't know very well.

Pops, as I sometimes called him, always carried a white cloth hankie in his pocket, and never went anywhere without his pocketknife. Before his retirement, Dad had worked as an electrician. His tan leather tool pouch was weathered, and he often carried it rather than wear it around his waist as it was designed for. He had a myriad of tools in all sizes and shapes. Many of the tools had red rubber grips on the handles that he had put on himself. You could buy the tools with the grips already on, but it was cheaper to do it yourself. As children, curiosity nearly paralyzed my sister and me as we stood in the kitchen near the stove and watched him put the rubber grips on. He dipped the bright red, rigid plastic tubes into boiling water until they were pliable, and then pulled them out with tongs and slid them onto the metal handles of pliers, wrenches, and screwdrivers. I knew I would never forget that color. Red, the perfect shade of red, became my favorite color.

Dad's barn was literally his second home. I think he thought of it as his refuge. I was about to find out it was not just Dad's hangout, I also discovered the barn was chock-full of birds. These birds evidently considered it their refuge, too. You might say they thought of it as their personal airstrip, where for many years they had been flying unhindered in and out of every crack in the old, weathered structure.

So after waking early this particular morning, I headed off to the barn with the intention of organizing my wares. I laid out my braided area rug in the center of the barn and preceded to set up a mock living room with my caramel-colored sofa, brown overstuffed chairs, television, lights, and knickknacks. There was a lot of bird activity overhead as I arranged and rearranged my ensemble. There seemed to be some kind of flight pattern developing. I noticed the longer I worked, the more frantic the birds' movements became. Invasion of their territory never even crossed my mind.

After several hours working, I stepped back to look at the space and was pleased to see it was looking similar to a movie set. Surrounded by tools, yard equipment, and cobwebs, I envisioned my little furniture grouping complete with working stereo and mood lighting as a spot where I could relax, watch a little tube, and have a semblance of a home away from home.

Meanwhile, the birds seemed really annoyed. Was it my imagination or were they actually dive bombing in my direction? I chalked it up to my overactive imagination.

But it turned out their dissatisfaction was not my imagination. It took no more than three days before these winged angels clearly voiced their displeasure on every item I owned. The mattress, appliances, and furniture slowly became whitewashed in a shade you might call bird bomber white. I knew I had met my enemy and, unfortunately, they had the home court advantage. Who knew birds defecated so frequently or in such mammoth amounts?

When Dad heard me complaining to Mom about the birds, he yelled from the other room, "I could have told you that was going to happen. Why the hell did you bring all that crap with you anyway?"

The man wasn't gracious, but he did have a point. I asked myself again for the hundredth time, "Why *did* I bring all that crap with me, and more importantly, why am I here?"

Chapter Thirty

M om seemed to become less involved in the daily routine as my sister and I became more involved in their lives. Each day she was increasingly acting more like a child instead of an adult and a spouse. She wasn't offering to cook or do the laundry, and showed no desire to make decisions about Dad's health. Her demeanor was beginning to perplex and aggravate me.

"What's up with Mom?" I asked my sister one day when she came by on her way home from work. She looked over at me with a puzzled gaze. "I'm surprised you haven't noticed. You know, she seems to be losing interest in everything, especially being any comfort to Dad. She's just not involved."

My sister drew a deep breath before she said, "Annie, I've wanted to say something to you about this but I don't want you to get upset." She took a seat on the couch and motioned for me to do the same. "I think you come on a little strong. Remember, Mom and Dad and I were handling all this when you were still in Florida. I know you mean well, but you're kinda bossy." I tried to interrupt but she held up her hand in a gesture that said 'let me finish.' "Sometimes your suggestions sound more like directives. Maybe that's why Mom's involvement has lessened."

Her words stung, and two emotions washed over me—anger and embarrassment. I chose the low road and decided to run with anger.

"You really think that's it?" I asked with the hair tingling on the back of my neck and a flushed feeling moving over my face.

"I think it might be."

"But they're not proactive. It drives me nuts. That's why I decided to come here to help. Were you aware of the huge abrasion that was discovered on Dad's back over a month ago?" I asked her, trying to keep the volume of my voice under control.

My anger had been unbridled when I'd found that months earlier, Dad had discovered a huge abrasion on his back. When the irritated area refused to heal, he finally went to the family doctor to have it checked out. No biopsy was done. Instead, he was sent home with some topical cream and no plans for a follow-up visit.

My sister acknowledged she knew about the incident.

I responded, "What the hell! I couldn't believe his doctor didn't do more. That spot was exactly behind the cancer in his lung! Didn't anyone suggest more tests? Didn't you wonder why it wasn't healing even with the cream?" I asked her. Before she could answer, I continued. "Do you know what Mom said when I asked her about this on the phone? She said, 'Well, we've gone to Dr. Smith for so many years. I just don't think your dad would go to another doctor. Plus, it doesn't help that we see him around town. I think he doesn't take us seriously when we're in his office. He talks to us like old drinking buddies, rather than patients.' I knew I was not very understanding with them during phone calls when, after their doctor appointments, I asked what the doctors had said and their responses were vague and inconclusive.

"I wanted to jump through the phone receiver and wring someone's neck. I was livid with them, Julie. You know I begged them, to no avail, to take a voice recorder to the appointments so they could listen to it again when they got home. Several times I even tried to directly phone the doctors' offices to get details on their findings, but as you know from your own attempts, they aren't willing to release medical information even to the children."

And this wasn't the first time I had been absolutely exasperated by their medical treatment or lack of. My dogs and cats received more thorough diagnoses from their vets than my parents did from their doctors. Each time I hung up the phone in frustration, I took a deep breathe and reminded myself that they were adults, even if they were not acting as I thought adults should. For the first time, I was beginning to understand the concept of parents becoming the children and the children becoming the adults. It was a strange and confusing turn of events.

"I think their doctor is a quack," I said.

"That may be true, but it's their decision, Annie. Give them a little space. They're set in their ways. Come here and give me a hug," she said as she put her arms around me. "You know they love us, but we both get pretty impatient with them. They're old farts. They're set in their ways. And as far as your relationship with Dad, the two of you need to work it out. This animosity has been going on for years. The two of you make everyone else uncomfortable and miserable with your squabbles. Get over it. He's never going to change. The two of you are so much alike. Did you think about this before coming home? I did. I wanted to say something to you, but Mom stopped me. She was afraid we would hurt your feelings."

My sister and I both had tears in our eyes.

"Don't get me wrong, Sis. We all appreciate you being here. But it's not necessary or expected that you provide all the solutions. We have to work together as a team, like we did when Mom was sick."

I knew she was right. I was acting like a human bulldozer—confrontational and headstrong. I also suddenly realized I had greatly underestimated the perplexity of being the parent to your parents, especially when you are still trying to learn to parent yourself.

Chapter Thirty One

"Dad, can I help you with that?" I asked as I spotted him in the garage struggling to pour dog food into a large metal bowl from the fifty-pound container he stored it in.

"Nope. I got it, Annie," he yelled over his shoulder.

Try as I might, he didn't often accept my help, and this time was no exception. Mom and I glanced at each other and shrugged. Stubbornness and independence were just part of who he was and always had been.

It was a ritual. Each morning at 7:30 on the nose, Hooper made her way to the corner of the garage where she took her post in anticipation of her daily meal, which usually consisted of a mixture of dry kibbles and tomatoes from Dad's garden, or any other wet concoction he could come up with. Dad called her waiting stance being on high alert.

"Look, Hoopie is on high alert. Guess its time for breakfast!" he would call out to no one in particular.

Dad passed on his love for dogs to my sister and me at a young age. We learned his rules of treating animals properly. Among those dictates was disdain for any owner who chained their dog outside. He believed anyone who chained a dog outside didn't deserve to have one. We got educated on home remedies like rubbing used motor oil on sores to heal a canine's itchy skin.

"Do you know how you can tell if a puppy is going to be smart?" Dad asked us each time one of our dogs had a litter or a neighbor got a new puppy. We knew the answer but we enjoyed the way he told it, so we always played dumb.

"No, Dad, how can you tell?"

"He will be the one that looks directly into your eyes when you talk to him or her. That will be the smart one when he grows up. You can count on it," Dad said. "Look at Hooper. There's never been a smarter dog. She looks right at you. She understands everything I say."

Dad wouldn't get any argument from us on this subject. Not only was Hooper a beautiful chocolate Labrador, she did appear to have quite an understanding of human vocabulary. As she was spoken to, she cocked her big brown head to the side as if she were processing the meaning of your words. On command, she would retrieve his shoes from the bedroom, pick a tomato from the garden and bring it to the house, and search endlessly until she found his little tin filled with chewing tobacco that he purposely hid from her.

"Hooper, go get my shoe," Dad would yell as he pointed toward the bedroom. In thirty seconds or less she would come galloping around the corner and drop the shoe at his feet. Sometimes it wasn't the right shoe and Dad would say to her, "No, not my work shoe. My house shoe. Go get my house shoe."

She never disappointed us. Returning with the right shoe, she brought a smile to Dad's face that was infectious. She was greeted with an adoring pat on the head as Dad removed the slobbery shoe from her mouth.

"Watch this one," Dad said. "Mom, go put my snuff can on top of the pool table."

My sister and I looked at each other as Mom hopped up and headed toward the garage. Mom was as obedient as the dog. In the garage she placed the snuff in its designated place while we all sat riveted to the sofa like we were watching a high-wire act at the circus.

128

"Hoop, go get my snuff. Go get it!" Dad commanded, and off she went on her quest. This search took a little longer. Her tail wagging furiously, she traveled from room to room and eventually to the garage where she made a lap around the pool table, stopped abruptly, rose up on her hind legs, and grabbed the snuff can right off the pool table. She ran happily back to us where she gave Dad the snuff, and where we gave her applause, hugs, and praise worthy of a king.

Dad was right. He had himself one smart animal. And this smart animal had herself one cushy home. We called her our family dog, but there was no doubt her loyalties were to Dad. She was his faithful and devoted companion who watched his every move. Hooper wasn't her original name, but Dad saddled her with it because he loved basketball and called the scoring process getting a hoop.

It was a man and his dog love affair, especially when Dad offered her a ride in his pickup truck. There were several times when she nearly ran through the closed screen door in her excitement. Most dogs ride in the bed of the truck, but not Hoop. Everyone in town was used to, and rather expected, to see her big brown head and floppy ears riding statuesquely in the passenger seat right next to Dad as he chauffeured her around.

Second in pleasure only to the truck rides were the rides on the four-wheeler. Dad called them rides, but he was actually the one who rode and she chased along beside him barking feverishly the whole time.

I enjoyed watched them zigzag across the neighboring fields and up and down the fencerows on the four-wheeler. Dad always wore a hat and a look of joy and freedom that maybe only a dog and his master can experience together. The sight always made me feel that all was right with the world - at least this tiny part.

Chapter Thirty Two

It turned out Mom's intuition about keeping her port was right on. Upon completion of Dad's radiation treatments, he and Mom both began another round of chemotherapy—his for his recent diagnosis, and Mom's as a follow-up to her cancer earlier in the year.

I couldn't help but think how odd it was that during a catastrophic illness the most unusual events can provide comfort. Chemo days, as Dad called them, were often looked forward to with a subdued enthusiasm like the local fish fry or a tournament basketball game would normally bring about. He was convinced, outwardly anyway, that chemo was the last leg before he defeated this ugly disease.

Both of my parents were having chemo today. It was an outing, and I was the official chauffeur. I had never before paid attention to buildings with the word oncology on them. How could I have missed them all? Now they seemed to appear on every other corner. This particular clinic had a covered entryway that reminded me of a church portico where the elderly get dropped off close to the door. I pulled into the portico and watched as my mom and dad got out of the car and pulled open the glass doors of the office. Mom turned to look back at me before I moved toward the parking lot. My heart raced and then broke again into little pieces, just as it did each time we made this trip. I brushed away a tear before I walked up to the clinic door, but I couldn't brush away the sadness that weighed me down.

Each of these visits provided Mom and me the opportunity to witness nothing short of a comedic, medical miracle. Grouchy and irritable on the drive there, the minute Dad was greeted by a nurse from the chemo suite he transformed into another persona.

Mom and I watched with disbelief, despite the fact we had witnessed it many times, as he became the laughing, jovial, super-friendly guy he was at a bar around his drinking buddies. He was a walking ray of sunshine in a room where most of the people were hooked up to machines pumping poison through their veins. The whole scene was surreal and felt to me like the intermission before the final act of a play. But Dad showed no signs of the negative emotions I was experiencing. I suspected his fear was just below the surface and I couldn't help but admire him, even though it aggravated me as well. His fortitude was remarkable as he shamelessly flirted with the nurses and they flirted back. It was as if he put on a happy mask.

There was one thing Mom and I knew for sure. The minute the appointment was over and we exited out the front door where there was no audience, the happy mask was disposed of in the nearest trash can and the authentic man reappeared. The real Dad was unfortunately, but understandably, still grouchy and even more irritable than before. We drove home in awkward silence and in the shadow of the two-faced man.

One pretty young nurse Dad had grown particularly fond of must have felt the same for him. Several months later after his treatments were completed and care became palliative in nature, she showed up at our house with a beautiful bouquet of flowers for him. Dad was at first embarrassed by her affection, but then couldn't hide his delight at the attention. We were all moved by her generosity and compassion. Obviously, my father's tender side, the one we so seldom saw, had touched her. After the nurse left, Dad went back to bed,

131

and my sister, Mom, and I gathered in the garage where we spoke in hushed tones and chuckled about 'Don Juan' Garold's charisma.

"Boy, he has her buffaloed," Mom said. "If she only knew what a rat he can really be."

"He has always known how to turn on the charm," I said, "when he wants to."

"Yes. And you know how he loves those flat little bellies, as he calls them," Mom retorted with sarcasm.

As I listened to her, I thought how odd it is that older people, having been married for so many years, can still be so jealous of one another. I told myself I would never be like that, knowing full well I already was. I considered jealousy one of my ugliest personality traits. Was it possible this kind of attitude was inherited? Maybe I had inherited my hard shell and sharp tongue from Dad, and my jealous nature from Mom. Accurate or not, it was nice to have someone to blame it all on.

Chapter Thirty Three

J ust as the sun surely rose every day, so too each morning the realization of our status quo hit me like a Florida rainstorm that shows up thundering out of nowhere in the middle of a cloudless day.

God, my Mom and Dad both have cancer, and I need a job.

"Annie, I worry about you driving into the city," Mom said as I prepared to leave for the dreaded job search.

We grew up only twenty miles outside "the City," the name Mom had given to the capital city and closest metropolitan area. It was the place she'd grown up in.

"I'll be all right, Mom. Don't worry about me. I always keep my car doors locked and walk like I mean business. I've heard walking like that is a deterrent to being attacked by someone."

"Well, just remember people aren't the same in the city as they are here," she yelled as she stood shivering at the garage door, waving good-bye to me.

Perhaps created by bad childhood memories or an abundance of local news stories covering crime and poverty that had enveloped most of the nation's metropolitan areas, her references to the city were negative and crawling with ominous warnings regarding safety issues.

I didn't have many childhood memories of trips into the city, only an occasional one to see a grandma or aunt. I did recall, however, the odor that filled the air once we neared the city limits. Even blindfolded I would have recognized where we were. It was a factory smell, heavy and smoky. The buildings looked ancient and were by far the biggest I had ever seen as a child. The sky always seemed to be gray there. I didn't particularly remember it being scary like Mom was now describing. I just recalled it being putrid and ugly.

It was my third day job searching. I was already over it, but I didn't have the heart to tell Mom that. She had enough other things to worry about.

After the expenses of the moving truck and Don's compensation for helping me with the move, I arrived in Indiana pretty much penniless. Just eight months sober, I was still reeling from the results of years of financial irresponsibility. I had grown accustomed to running from uncomfortable situations and falling back on help from Mom and Dad. This time my situation was finances and sick parents, both of which supplied me with a reason for a geographic cure. In my heart, I knew it was part of the reason I had decided to pack up and return to Indiana. I also suspected I was looking for moral support, and a few bucks again in my time of need.

It wasn't long before I found a snag in this plan. My dad was so ill, I didn't have the nerve or heart to ask him for money. He didn't need one more concern dished onto his plate. Mom would sneak me a few dollars here and there, but it wasn't enough to keep me afloat until I came up with another source.

Before leaving Florida, I convinced myself it would be easy to find employment once I arrived in Indiana. But Indiana didn't cooperate. After a mountain of applications and reams of resumes, I still didn't have a job. Overqualified, underqualified, or too old, it just wasn't happening. I finally found hope at a temporary agency. Mom and Dad surely wouldn't approve though—all their job placements were in the dreaded big city. After a few typing tests, the agency found a job for me.

Most participants in a recovery program will tell you that healing the inside is the only sure way to heal the outside. Part of that process for me was overcoming the scars of an infamously short stint in a Bible college, and wiping out the memories of what I saw as a rigid, religious sect bound by monastic rules and people who led dull lives because they were not allowed to dance, gamble, drink, or curse for the fear of going to hell. It seemed to me His people (God's people, that is) didn't have any fun. But maybe God did have a sense of humor, a perverted one, because me, the nonbeliever and Bible college dropout, received my first job assignment. I would be working in a church, and I was freaked.

The day before my assignment started, I made a trip to the church. This was not just any church. It was a huge, prestigious church in the wealthiest section of the city. The property and building alone left me breathless the first time I saw it. Set in the rolling hills of a neighborhood of palatial residences, it was monumental in architectural scope alone. The autumn weather had worked her magic on the surrounding trees and foliage, transforming them into a palette of gold and burnt orange. The setting looked like a scene on a picture postcard. With multiple steeples rising majestically from a sprawling three stories of intricately designed limestone, standing in the parking lot I felt like a tiny, heathen church mouse in a great maze.

On my drive back to my parents' house, I found myself asking, What does one wear on the first day of a new job? I thought I was an old pro at this wardrobe thing since I'd had plenty of practice (it felt like a million times) preparing for the first day at a new position. But in this case, it needed to be something that was church appropriate. I eliminated all the short, low-cut, or devilishly garish printed garments now crammed into the very same closet where my Jesus-period attire had hung during high school.

Always restless and searching for some purpose even at a young age, I had helped to form a prayer group in high school. The religious activities filled some need in me. The Jesus Freaks, as we called ourselves, met on the stage every Thursday morning before school started. Seated in a circle, we read from the Bible and prayed. Our meetings caused quite a stir among the student body and faculty. I heard some of the adults muttering something about separation of church and state, but I had no idea what they were talking about, and I didn't really care. I enjoyed the commotion. The more the uproar, the better I liked it.

I found Jesus stickers and plastered them everywhere. I even wore them on the heels of my shoes. But like my Bible college adventure, which would come a few years later, the high school prayer sessions quickly whimpered into history, leaving not a single sign of their existence behind.

As an adult, I was used to faking the skills part of a job. I had made a career of applying for jobs for which I was not qualified. But here at my new job at the church, I felt like I was faking not just the skills, but the religious part, too. My responsibilities included many computer projects that I had no idea how to accomplish, and I depended on my fellow workers to guide me. One of those workers was a woman named Joy.

Joy seemed intent on questioning me about the circumstances of my moving back to Indiana. She had a daughter and was blunt about saying that as much as she loved her parents, she would never leave her child behind like I had, regardless of the circumstances. There was something about her I liked, even though her directness and disapproval made me cringe.

Much to my surprise, I found the backside of running a large church was just like running any big business in the secular community. For employment here no religious affiliation was required. No one in the office was particularly religious, nor were many of them even members of the congregation. The only concerns were your typing speed and your preference for pizza or subs for lunch. I was relieved no one asked or cared if you prayed. God was only in the minute details here, and that was a relief to me.

After a few days at the new job, I got brave enough to explore a little outside my cubicle. Winding down a few hallways, where my steps sounded thunderous on the polished marble floors and past the glow of stained-glass windows awash in the midday sun, I came upon a small chapel. It reminded me of one of the things I most regretted leaving behind in Florida—the Saint Francis chapel. Tucked on a little side street near downtown Fort Lauderdale, the Saint Francis chapel, part of a men's halfway house, had become a refuge for me after I discovered it during a recovery meeting that was held next door. Dark and musty, the chapel consisted of a small, narrow space defined by old and dirty red carpeting, dark wooden pews separated by one aisle, and a handmade wooden cross hung at the opposite end furthest from the entry door. The entire space was only about ten feet wide and dimly lit by a few low-watt bulbs. It was crazy, but I found it was the only place I could even attempt to pray, and a twelve step program had convinced me that praying was an intricate part of a successful recovery from any kind of addiction. In times of despair and happiness, of which I'd had many during my early recovery, I found myself going there searching for serenity and some measure of understanding of a higher power. It crossed my mind that maybe it wasn't just a coincidence that I'd found another special place right here in the middle of this Indiana church among all the godliness I so feared.

I started arriving at work a little earlier in the morning so I could spend a few moments in the back pew of the chapel. Alone with my thoughts, and I hoped the rapt attention of some higher power, I prayed for help in the journey that my parents and I were involuntarily taking together. In spite of myself, I could feel just a little of my fear come to the surface and lessen each time.

Chapter Thirty Four

It has been my experience that all homes have a distinct smell. Mom and Dad's certainly did. Each time I walked in the back door, the scent transported me in a time machine right back to childhood. The aroma was a mixture of cigarette smoke, well water, dog, and Old Spice – my dad's favorite cologne. The overall scent wasn't exactly pleasant, but it was home. It made me feel like I'd never left.

It's funny how 'home' never really changes. One of my favorite artists, Brian Andreas wrote, "Whenever I go on a trip I think about all the homes I've had and remember how little has changed about what comforts me." Our childhood bedrooms barely looked like my sister and I had ever left. I was perhaps the only thing that had changed in all these years. The paint and carpeting were the same, and I would be getting dressed in the very room thirty years later without missing a beat.

Dad had just finished cutting the lawn when I got home. The sweet smell of cut grass was a home smell as well. Mom was grilling steaks, and Dad was reading the last of a pile of newspapers that lay in front of him before taking the dog for a truck ride. I'd found myself in a race with a beautiful Midwestern sunset as I drove home.

I had just finished laying out my church clothes for tomorrow's workday when I heard some commotion going on in the living room. My dad's youngest brother Jerry had dropped by. It only took a glance to see he wasn't in great shape. He was "three sheets to the wind" as Dad called it. My uncle didn't drink often but he was sure a mess this evening. It was no secret he was taking Dad's illness about as hard as any of us, and like the rest of the Limp men, drunkenness was how he was letting off steam.

Dad and his three brothers didn't get together often, but when they did, the scene was predictable. Friendly and social at first, the tension would mount with the opening of each beer bottle. The drunker they got, the more honest they became. The old wounds and resentments bubbled up like raw sewage coming out of an overworked septic tank. What usually ensued was not pretty or brotherly.

One of these incidents occurred while I was still in grade school. This time the reunion of sorts wasn't the normal occasion of funeral, graduation, or birthday like it usually was. The brothers had gathered to see our new house.

I heard loud, drunken voices coming from the garage. What started as a friendly game of pool had turned into a nasty shouting match. I could hear Mom trying to intervene and calm the voices down. Dad's oldest brother left in a huff. Little did we know that a short time later he would return with a gun threatening all of them. There was a standoff in the front yard where they all stood frozen in disbelief as the one brother waved the gun in the air. I don't know where the strength or the idea came from, but I charged out of the front door of the house swinging a huge cast iron frying pan above my head and screaming, "I will kill all of you."

With the advantage of hindsight, I can only surmise that the sight of an enraged little girl swinging a weapon from the kitchen jolted them into a moment of sober clarity, and they all scattered and went home. Afterward, not a detail of the night was ever mentioned again. Now here we were years later—much older brothers, but maybe no wiser. My heart ached for my Uncle Jerry who was trying to make sense out of Dad's cancer and fears of his own mortality.

The next morning as I headed out for my job, I tiptoed past my uncle where he had spent the night on our couch. I knew he would wake up hungover and humiliated. I could hear the words of my recovery sponsor who reminded me that alcohol only adds to the sadness one is drinking to forget about.

Chapter Thirty Five

One night after returning home from work, I helped Mom with the dinner dishes and then headed off to my bedroom to continue sorting through boxes of old stuff that I had discovered since inhabiting my old room. There was my first grade photograph showing the uneven cut Mom had given my bangs. The camera had accurately captured my look of embarrassment and horror.

Several high school yearbooks were there, too. Students had written the standard sentiments on the front and back inside covers. "You're the best. Good luck in all you do!" "To my best friend ever! I will miss you!" I laughed as I read through the comments, pausing at each name and trying to connect it to a face. There were a few my memory had lost with time, but most I could picture as if I'd seen them yesterday instead of thirty-some years ago.

As I pulled out boxes, I thought back to some of the television shows I'd seen on hoarders. I didn't classify myself as one, and Mom wasn't your typical hoarder, either, but she did hang on to items that most people probably would have thrown away. I realized I had inherited some of that tendency from her.

Occasionally, digging through boxes or drawers looking for a specific item, my sister and I found our pacifiers, baby teeth, even locks from our first haircuts. Also among the found treasures was a newspaper article showing a picture of our red terrier dog named Amber who had adopted two baby ducklings. I had completely forgotten about retail stores, or dime stores as we called them, that used to sell baby chicks, ducklings, and turtles with painted shells at Easter time. More shocking was that parents used to buy these little creatures for their children. In this case, my sister and I picked out two little ducks, and when we brought them home, our dog had assumed the role of mother and crawled right into the cardboard box with them. Like she had with her litter of puppies, she rolled on her side to allow them to nurse and the little ducks pecked at her teats just like they knew what they were doing.

Our local newspaper must have been short on news for that day's edition and responded to our call with an interview and a photo for the evening edition. We were delighted when we saw it in print, and Amber became a star. The ducks? They lived to a ripe old age, for ducks anyway, with one even surviving a broken leg when one of our Shetland ponies stepped on her. We doctored her up by making a splint out of a Popsicle stick and taped it onto her leg. She recovered nicely. And sure enough, right there in the box of memorabilia was the very splint with duck feathers still attached. Our family truly threw absolutely nothing away.

I continued to root through the boxes finding old concert ticket stubs and high school play bills for our production of the musical *Music Man* and the drama *Our Town*. It was all there, brown and crinkled with age. In spite of her grumbling about all the space the boxes consumed, I was grateful Mom had kept them all these years.

Mom came into the bedroom a couple of times and laughed when she saw the mess I was making. As I pulled each item out and piled everything up around me, the trip down memory lane led me late into the night. Just as I was about to abandon the boxes until tomorrow, I came across a diary I had started in my sophomore year of high school. It was a royal blue color and the treasured kind a teenager loves—the kind with a lock. Of course the lock had long ago broken, so I flipped it open and discovered it was empty. My disappointment was short lived though as I realized there were a few lines of writing on the first page. It was the sole entry. It read:

I want Dad to be my hero. I desperately need him to be my hero.
Every life desire is second to the longing of this affirmation.
Can I find it by impressing him with my knowledge? Can I earn his validation?
Can I find his affection? Can I steal his love?
Can I be still enough to see behind his impenetrable wall?
I continue to search for a chink in his suit of armor.
I know he has a compassionate and sentient soul. I believe that's where mine comes from.
I am driven by the hunt to ferret the emotions out of him.
Hope appears and then is smashed again, and again.
I am momentarily idled by futile attempts to scratch beneath his surface
But I can't give up the quest.
Even before the blood on my fingers has dried,
I start to claw at the metal armor again.

I closed the diary and sat in stunned silence. I tried to convince myself I'd written these disturbing words for an English assignment or some other project. But I knew that wasn't the truth. The words were my reality. Sadness swept over me like the steam in a sauna. I looked down again at the words I had written long ago about my dad. I wasn't really surprised, and yet they startled me. I asked myself if it was possible to love and hate someone at the same time. They were like the emotions between us the day in the truck when I had slapped him. The day I wanted to run and never look back.

I recalled that after that night, and for the next several weeks, I had camped out at my sister's house—a refuge away from the man I thought I was home to help. One minute I had been sad and crying, the next I was angry and anxious.

When I finally returned to Mom and Dad's house after that incident, Dad and I never again spoke of that day and what had gone on between us, but the dark shadow of the moment was there nonetheless. It followed us from room to room, breathing heavily and sullen-like. It reminded me of one of my favorite television shows from when I was in junior high school, *Dark Shadows* starring Barnabas Collins. It was an eerie show about tormented souls. Our lives could have been the sequel to that show, starring father and daughter.

Unfortunately, I knew better. I knew the value of diary entries, the depth of complicated feelings that can exist just beneath the surface of a few simple thoughts. I knew this because my mother always kept a diary.

Mom's diaries were the five-year kind. They had the day of the month at the top of each page and space for the next five years on that date below it. I didn't know what time of the day she usually wrote in them. I never saw her doing it so I assumed it was early in the morning before everyone else woke up. She wrote her name, address, and phone number on the inside of every front cover. There were five or six of her older diaries stacked in the hall closet. My sister often called her when a date was in question.

"Mom, what year did Amber get her contact lenses?" "What year did Grandpa Otto die?"

Mom could always find the answer for us. She wrote about the weather, phone calls to her kids, and the robins.

Monday, February 24, 1992
53 degrees – a little sun. Just talked to Julie. She sounds awful. It's hard to have to work when you're that sick. Robins and Doves are mating already.

Sunday, May 31, 1992

1ˢᵗ ripe tomato! Dad is so proud. He beat out all his friends.

Monday, June 1, 1992

76 degrees. Garold doesn't deserve a good b-day. He's a bastard. No one should be nice to him and I mean it. Sometimes I think there's something wrong with his brain. One mood after another.

Thursday, February 10, 1994

Some sun. 21 degrees so the snow didn't melt. Garold can't get outside and he is like a caged lion pacing back and forth. He's driving me nuts.

Friday, July 8, 1994

88 degrees. Cool down this weekend. I'm glad this O.J. thing is over. Garold out til 1:30 a.m.

Friday July 9, 1994

Took off and spent the day with Mary Jo. Came home, Garold was drunk again. I give up. He didn't have any reason for this.

Tuesday, May 14, 1996

60 degrees and sunny. Made a nice pot roast.

Tuesday, July 30, 1996

Good day til Lee and Dad had a few words. She went to Julie's house and stayed the night. Oh boy.

Friday, August 2, 1996
Boring day. Robins are gone already.

Mom wrote about the things that were important to her, and some days she just wrote, "Nothing much to say" or "Feeling blah." It was seldom that she left a page blank. On the last page before the inside cover there was a long list of dates. The dates were in three-month increments and were of supreme importance to her. They were the dates she received her infamous permanents at the beauty parlor.

One of the consistencies in Mom's diaries was always an entry on December 31, New Year's Eve, of each year. She summed up the previous 364 days with comments like:

1989 "It's been a good year. Thank you, Lord."
1992 "Goodbye '92."
1994 "Turbulent year, but thank you anyway, Lord."
1998 "What a year this has been. Too ugly to write about."

Sitting there on the bedroom floor, surrounded by pieces of my past, I closed her diary and had to wonder what Mom would write about at this year's end. Sickness, maybe death. Who knew if she would even have the heart or strength to write anything.

Chapter Thirty Six

I was grateful Friday evening had finally arrived. It had been a long week. During dinner it dawned on me that it had been several days since Dad had gotten the four-wheeler out of the barn. That was unusual so I asked him if he needed help.

"Hey, Dad. You want me to take Hoop on the four-wheeler?"

"I think she'd like that." He looked over at his four-legged friend and said, "What do you say, girl? Are you ready to hit the four-wheeler?"

Hooper answered by jumping up and down and prancing around in circles. She was ready!

I was surprised and happy Dad had agreed to let me help. Off to the barn we headed. She lead the way but kept looking back to make sure I was following her. I turned to look back toward the house and saw Dad watching us from the patio doors. I felt a lump form in my throat as I realized he hadn't forgotten to take her for the last few days, he just didn't have enough energy to do it. The sting of reality hurt.

As Hoop and I maneuvered up and down the dormant crop rows, I was reminded once again how beautiful the countryside can be. In summer, the fields have a color palette of golden wheat and the deep green of soybeans reaching up to the sun. In winter, with the crops gone, the fields lay quietly at rest. In this dormant state they reminded me of an old black and white film filling an outdoor theater with dramatic silence, except now the silence was broken with the barking of one happy, tail-wagging, mud-slinging pooch.

There was something peaceful and comforting about the acreage of unplanted parcels around my parents' house. Maybe because it was familiar territory, the fields brought about a sense of serenity for me, a condition I didn't often feel. I could remember the smell of the freshly tilled soil in the spring, and how it looked so black and rich. Then the aroma changed in the fall to the smell of dried corn and parched dirt.

The whir of the farm equipment rolling along was a huge part of the soundtrack of my childhood. I was sure it had been a part of Dad's childhood, too. It was hard to think of Dad as a vulnerable little boy, but it helped to think of him that way. It helped me to recognize, at least a little, that we treat others as we have been treated, and we don't know what we don't know. I was pretty sure he had only passed on to his children what he had been given as a child.

I looked back again toward the house and Dad was still standing at the patio door watching Hoop and me. The sight gave me the same feeling I had when I read the last page of a great novel. Like in every book, the end of the story is inevitable, but sometimes you're just not ready for the last chapter.

I wasn't prepared for the end of this story.

Chapter Thirty Seven

As the days passed and most of my care-giving efforts were failing miserably, I decided to try a philosophic approach. Reading the deepening depression on my dad's face, I appointed myself the Dr. Phil of the household. I left Dad little notes of inspiration and hope in obscure places where he would least expect to find them: a note under his pillow—"Sweet dreams, Dad."; a quote in a small wooden box where he kept his snuff and his pocketknife—"Today is the first day of the rest of your life."; an inspirational pamphlet about surviving cancer in his magazine rack in the bathroom.

I waited for him to acknowledge my efforts. His silence about the discoveries felt like approval to me, so I worked harder to provide him with frequent written messages of encouragement. But I was wrong about his acceptance. I was either naive or I'd forgotten how he could use his silence to conceal his anger and disapproval.

One evening when a trivial discussion between us became heated, the veil was lifted and his anger spilled over like the lid on a pot that has long before started to boil.

"I just watched a news report about how many states still don't recognize the Martin Luther King, Jr. holiday." I knew the minute the last word left my lips and I looked at his wrinkled brow that I had blundered big time. He didn't like the topic and used the opportunity to vent about the origin of his bottled-up anger.

"I don't care what you think," he yelled at me. "What the hell are you trying to prove? And what's with these notes everywhere? Enough already."

He let me know he viewed my notes of encouragement as vile and intrusive. He loved them about as much as one would like rabbit droppings left randomly throughout the house by a pet bunny. I was once again reminded of why as a child I had spent so many hours locked safely away in my bedroom. It dawned on me again that no one had really invited me here. It was his home, after all. I felt childish, embarrassed, and riddled with shame. I could mark those notes of encouragement off the to-do list, too. This realization jogged memories of the notes Dad had left for us years ago.

Mom and I would often find his notes lying on the kitchen table when we woke up in the morning. There it would be—usually written in pencil on a scrap of paper—the apologetic attempt to redeem himself from his actions the night before.

"Sorry, Mom. Please wake me @ 7:00. Love, Dad"
"You know I love you, Annie. Sorry. Dad"

The notes made me want to scream at him. What are you sorry for? Your anger? Your impatience? Your judgment and cruel words?

On many of the nights right before these notes had been written, Dad would make an attempt to apologize before he passed out. I would hear him drunkenly swaying in my bedroom doorway and whispering, "Annie. Annie, are you awake?" And like the games of hopscotch or jump rope one is supposed to be learning at an early age, I learned to play possum. Lying perfectly still, I held my breath until I heard him walk away from my room. I told myself I didn't want to hear anything he had to say, at least not while he was drinking. But as soon as I knew the coast was clear, the tears came. I wanted his affection, his approval, and his attention. Why couldn't he give them when he was sober?

While he stood at my door, I could hear the remorse in his voice. I tried convincing myself he meant well. The truth was his notes actually hurt more than the conflict that had prompted their writing. I was sure Mom probably felt the same way. Sometimes it seemed it wasn't really us he hated, but that he hated himself. For some reason, I intuitively recognized this state of mind. It was caused by misdirected anger and, unfortunately, I knew all about that kind of anger.

Chapter Thirty Eight

The house was quiet except for the low volume of the evening news on television. Dad had gone to bed early, and Mom and I had settled on staying home for dinner. As she made our sandwiches, she mentioned the neighbors had gone to Hawaii on vacation.

"I know you've always wanted to go to Hawaii, Mom. I'm sorry you haven't made it there. I don't remember us taking family vacations. Did we?"

I didn't mention it right then, but I was still struggling to retrieve some good memories from the past. I found myself asking if it's possible some people only remember the bad moments? I certainly didn't want to be one of those unfortunate folks, but I couldn't dredge up anything but bad memories.

"Well, yes, honey. We took a few trips, although what we called a vacation was usually just a trip to the lake. Remember we had a cabin and a pontoon boat at Lake Lemon for a while," she said.

"I'd forgotten about the pontoon. I remember you and Dad called it the party boat. You guys had a lot of fun back then, didn't you?"

Being back home was beginning to help me confirm a suspicion I'd had for some time. It was the realization that as a child, I'd often felt like I was on the outside looking in at the world. It had taken years of upheaval and hindsight to recognize how often I assumed this perspective. Even as an adult, I was still drawn to looking in windows at what I imagined others lives to be like.

Sometimes as a youngster riding in the car at night, the warm glow of light from the interior of a house would give me the message that this was not just a house like our family had. This was a home. I ached for that warmth that my imagination told me was behind those walls. A number of parked cars clustered outside a house meant a party or family gathering inside. I didn't know what these gatherings felt like, but I wanted them anyway. I coveted the imagined activities and emotions I thought lay out of my reach, just as I had yearned in second grade for my classmate Susie's long blonde hair, or in fourth grade for my best friend Ellen's perfect handwriting.

I didn't talk about these feelings. The pain was too great. I knew in my heart that everyone would think I was embarrassingly weak. Besides, I was sure of the response Dad would fire my way. It was the same line we always heard whenever one of us had the wants, as he called them.

"Shit in one hand and wish in the other, and see which one fills up the fastest." Thanks Dad.

"It's a shame you don't remember more of the good times. I don't understand why. We did have fun sometimes," Mom said. "Remember how we used to turn the music up loud some nights and your dad would try to do the Twist. He was horrible and we laughed until we cried. Remember how we all danced together?" she asked, her eyes in a quizzical squint.

"Yeah, I do remember that. We had that small radio that had the worst sound."

"There you go with the bad stuff again," Mom said as she headed into the living room. "Do you remember how much you and Julie enjoyed it when Dad blew rings with his cigarette smoke? Oh, and do you remember how he would pull up his shirt and make his stomach look like a face that was laughing? I remember that like it was yesterday! Wonder if Dad still remembers?" Mom asked as she walked to the garage.

I looked out at the sun setting on a beautiful plowed field in the distance as I tried to sort out my thoughts. I remembered the times Mom was talking about, but I remembered them so differently.

My memories of family times, though rare, were magical. There were good nights, usually after Mom and Dad had a few drinks. We'd turn the music up loud, sing at the top of our voices, and dance in the living room. It was a moment like this when I first recognized the sensation of separating from myself. There was one of me involved in the moment, dancing and acting crazy, and one of me watching and recording the event like a documentary photographer who is present, but only from behind his camera lens.

These were the nights when I fell asleep almost a carefree child, hoping the magic would not disappear before the next morning. Some things could be counted on. Easter morning and the Easter bunny always arrived. On Christmas morning, Santa had always been there. But often on the mornings after our night of family fun, I learned there wasn't much to be counted on. Disappointment stung anew as soon as I awakened to loud, angry voices, or shivered from the icy pale that had descended upon the household. It didn't take long to figure out that the magic was gone. Maybe it had moved on to someone else's house—perhaps to one of those houses where the warm glow shone through the windows—but it had surely vanished from ours.

Mom and I said good night to each other. I could hear Dad snoring and hoped that meant he was sleeping restfully. As for me, I tossed and turned, willing the good memories to return. Later that night I dreamed I was on the pontoon boat trying to escape someone who was angry and chasing me. After my first sip of coffee the next morning, I realized with a start that the man in my dream had looked a lot like my dad.

Chapter Thirty Nine

It was a busy morning at work. Preparations for the church Christmas services were well underway. I was swamped with projects.

"Annie, are you dating anyone?" my coworker Joy asked.

My first impulse was to quickly respond, "No. Do you know of anyone?" but I didn't want to seem too eager so I kept my voice as calm as possible.

Early recovery had given me the chance to repeat, unfortunately, many of my mistakes one more time. There had been a few casual relationships since I'd gotten sober but nothing worth pursuing. I was still stinging from the one before I entered treatment, the one that had led me to picking up a drink again after thirteen years of abstaining. It had been a real heartbreaker.

Tainted from the beginning with two drunks uniting, it was one of the most passionate, unhealthy affairs I'd ever encountered. Every foul characteristic I possessed came to life, including jealousy and rage. The more we drank, the more jealous I became. The longer I drank, the more argumentative I became. Between blackouts and physical violence, I became the drunk that even the other drunk couldn't tolerate.

In an alcohol-induced fog, any speck of self-respect I might have possessed was buried in guilt, shame, and remorse. I tried relentlessly, to no avail, to grovel my way back into the relationship. Trying to let go of it took me to the brink of a mental breakdown and a fearful state of mind that I'd never experienced before. At a jumping off place, as recovery programs coin it, I couldn't live with alcohol or without it. The relationship and the bottle had me circling the drain. It was then that I scraped the money together by borrowing against my home and headed out of the country to a treatment center.

One of the most precious gifts of sobriety that I was experiencing was the opportunity to look at the wrong turns I had taken in the past, accept my part in each debacle, and choose to make the same mistake again or take a different, healthier path.

I was just beginning to recognize that I had no clue of the real meaning of commitment. My three unsuccessful marriages proved that fact. In each case, a string of bad moods, illogical thinking, and impulsive decisions moved my relationships toward an ugly demise. I never let anyone too close. Vulnerability was a closed door. I weed-whacked my way through one friendship after another with both males and females. Heaps of dead soldiers lined the path behind me. I knew I wasn't unique in mistaking sex for love, but the frequency of my amorous endeavors left me with little hope or self-esteem. I often heard that many in recovery don't have relationships—we take hostages. I knew this was true, but I questioned my strength to heed those wise words.

As soon as Joy finished asking the question, I rolled my chair back and looked into the cubicle where she had her cell phone up to her ear like she did most of the time. A few minutes later she hung up her phone and said she had a guy she wanted me to meet.

"I'm meeting up with a few people tonight," she said. "We're going to meet at a pub over by the courthouse. It's called the Legal Beagle. We go there all the time. Why don't you come meet us and I'll introduce you to him. By the way, he doesn't drink either."

Even though this mystery man didn't drink, I wasn't crazy about the pub idea. I did like the name, though, and coming back into the city at night might be fun. Besides, it would be great to have a break from watching detective shows all evening with Mom and Dad. That evening after work, I made excuses to my parents about plans I had made and back into the city I went.

Joy and I arrived at the pub about the same time. It was located in the heart of downtown near all the government buildings and courts, thus the name I guessed. From the outside it wasn't too impressive, but inside it was full of life. Lit from behind, the stained glass behind the bar gave it the feel of an old English pub. The dark plank floor creaked as you walked. I felt a warm flush of comfort and excitement wash over me. It was like the feeling of the first drink and a sensation I hadn't experienced in a while.

Joy and I found a seat in a corner by the front window and had just started to chat when he walked our way. Actually, he was swaggering our way. He wore tight faded jeans, a baseball cap on backward, and the smile of a fox just entering the chicken coop. He was strikingly tall and thin. Joy embraced him and then turned to introduce him to me. His name was Dennis, and as my father would say, he was as black as the ace of spades.

Perhaps it is human nature to be fascinated by the unfamiliar. I had known few black people, but I had never had one as a close friend, and certainly not an articulate, attractive black man. Dennis was all of these. His wit was disarming, his intellect exuberating. I had never known a criminal defense attorney. Hell, in all honestly, I didn't even know black people went to law school.

He pulled up a stool beside me. I felt the heat from his beautiful black body and his piercing black eyes. However, just as powerful was the image of my father's face that appeared before me and the sound of his scorn ringing in my ears. I thought of the painting of the Last Supper that hung at my Grandma's house. And I wasn't Jesus hosting the dinner party. I was Judas. All thoughts of consequences were doused by lust. I fell in love with Dennis before he even finished his first sentence.

Chapter Forty

The frequency of my drives into the city doubled once I met Dennis. He and I often had lunch during work days and met on the weekends as well. Mom was curious about my extracurricular activities and asked a lot of questions, which I tried to artfully dodge with all the honesty I could muster. My nerves were frayed, though, because Mom always had the knack of reading between the lines when it came to my moods and emotions. I knew I was weaving a complicated and dangerous web, but I was stuck in it like the fly that falls prey to the spider.

"What do you do in the city? Your sister said she meets you there sometimes. Are these all people you work with at the church? I worry about you and Julie driving up there. Is she going with you tonight?" Mom asked.

"Not tonight, Mom. She said she's too tired. Sometimes we just play cards or just hang out when we're there," I explained. I gave her some details about the pub and that a lot of attorneys hung out there. These tidbits of information seem to placate her curiosity, at least until my next trip.

I soon discovered Mom was accurate when she described downtown Indianapolis as very different from our rural area. Although I didn't take her warnings as seriously as she thought I should, I recognized I was frequenting a place where you did lock the doors and look over your shoulder. It was definitely not Johnson County.

Chapter Forty One

Our part of the country was a patchwork of small farms and one stoplight towns, and our little town was no exception. On my drive to work I noticed most of the homes, except for the occasional housing development, were part of a farming parcel, or at least had a barn or silo, or both, on the property. The scenery being so unlike South Florida, reminded me that Dad's family, and most generations before, crafted their living like the majority of the community at the time, working the land and selling the corn, wheat, and soybeans they harvested.

The drive from my parents' home into the city each day was like taking a silent trip in a time machine. It began along cornfields and large parcels of land where small white farmhouses had been passed down from one generation to another with little or no changes or improvements. The early morning country roads were lined with weathered barns, John Deere tractors at rest in the fields, and metal mailboxes along the roadside mounted on wooden poles, worn and bent from their last encounter with a reckless driver who veered too close to the embankment.

I loved the aerial sight of this part of the country that I had enjoyed many times from an airplane. From above, the ground looked like a display of precisely chiseled squares of many colors. It was nature's quilt. The closer my drive took me toward the metropolitan area, the patchwork of farmland slowly gave way to suburbia where SUVs filled driveways and two story brick houses were tightly clustered into neighborhoods with cul-de-sacs.

Looking out the car window at the beginning of my drive to work, rural life looked simple, sleepy, and pretty plain. Expensive frills and fine cars were nowhere to be found. These were the homes of working people, eeking out modest livings, and whose daily routines included trips to the grocery and hardware stores, and church on Sunday. I saw nothing more, nothing less, and nothing else.

Well, there was the occasional turkey shoot. Dad had been going to them early on Sunday mornings since I was young. I thought they shot turkeys and was baffled when he always came home with a ham. It wasn't until I was an adult that I learned it was target practice, and turkeys and hams were given as prizes. I guess this was considered entertainment for country folks.

Dad's demeanor seemed to lighten on the rare occasions when we could persuade him to talk about his childhood and growing up as a country boy. And since my sister and I longed to see that side of him, we thoroughly enjoyed his stories, even when we'd heard them before.

One of the nice parts of growing up in a rural area was that the surroundings don't change much. You can drive the same roads year after year and everything is the same. There were very few new houses, and for that matter, seldom any new paint on the houses, either. That consistency, and the fact that Dad had grown up in the area, made it feel like our part of the country.

Very near our childhood home was a crossroad named 75W. After a few brews, and when Dad thought I was old enough to hear the story, he recounted a tale of his high school experience on 75W.

"You know when I was in high school, this was a make-out spot. See that area right there," he said as we passed by what appeared to be a just a dirt path, "We used to pull in there when we had a date and do a little smooching."

I laughed as I covered my face with my hands. I couldn't believe he was telling me this story.

"One night I was parked in there with my date when a farmer in a truck pulled in behind me with his bright lights on. It scared the crap out of me because he had us blocked in and I didn't have anywhere to drive to."

"What happened?" I asked.

"Well, he just rolled his window down and yelled that it was private property and to get the hell out of there."

"Did you ever go to that spot again?"

"Of course. Probably on my next date. When it was girl versus farmer, who do you think won out?"

We both laughed, and the rest of the way home I tried to imagine my dad on a date.

At the end of 75W there was one house we passed by often on our way home. The house wasn't anything out of the ordinary, just a typical small farmhouse, but there was a yard adornment like no other we'd ever seen. On the corner of the property, near the road, sat a rock, a big rock. It had a smooth surface, and was nearly three feet high and two feet wide. It was the perfect shape of a penis. Rumor was that it drew visitors from far and wide, and especially students from the local high school. Once you got your driver's license, it was like a rite of passage to drive your friends past the dick rock, as we called it. Dad pointed out that the dick rock had been there even when he was in high school. We wondered if the homeowners were aware they had a phallic sculpture on their property.

I remember thinking it was kind of an odd conversation for a dad and his daughter to have, but it was nice to see Dad joking around about anything since he didn't do it often, at least not with me. Once my sister and I heard Dad call it the dick rock, too, we delighted in using the name as often as possible, yelling it out every time we drove by. "There's the dick rock!" we would yell in unison.

161

Dad described his father's piece of farming land as very small compared to other farmers' parcels. Therefore his dad also raised chickens in order to make ends meet. Dad told a story that brought us to tears every time he recounted it.

During his teenage years, the family dog was a German shepherd named Rusty. Rusty had just shown up one day and adopted them as his family as so many strays or drop offs do when you live in the rural countryside.

Dad's parents were going out of town for several days and they left him and his brothers home to watch over things. Among his dad's money-producing crops were his chickens, several hundred of them. Sometime during those two days, the chickens discovered a small hole in the corner of the pasture fence. One by one they made their escape. These activities did not escape Rusty's attention. He was, after all, a shepherding dog by nature, and in his effort to shepherd them all back to where they belonged, he ran each and everyone of them to death, and then neatly placed them in two large piles right next to the hole in the fence. We squealed with anticipation and laughter as Dad described Grandpa's reaction when he discovered his lifeless crop of hens.

"I know my dad wanted to kill that dog, but how could he be mad at him? He had just done what he thought was his job," Dad explained. "After Grandpa got over the shock, we began to notice a change in Rusty's demeanor. Dare I say he was a little more confident and even cocky? For days afterward, he would go back to the spot where he had left the fruits of his labors piled high and smell around looking for them. Then looking very content and proud of himself, he would curl up and take a long nap. Grandpa swore that dog was very proud of himself and maybe he was," said Dad as he headed out the back door to the barn.

Dad's older and only sister, Louese, was a dainty, soft-spoken lady with curly brown hair and the quietest voice I'd ever heard. She was by far the most religious in our family. I was horrified one day as she smiled with satisfaction and described in vivid detail how she could wring the neck of a chicken in one swift movement. After she'd left and I'd recovered from the shock, I mentioned it to Dad. He reminded me that farm animals are raised for food. "When it's time to eat, their lives end," he said.

One of my school friends who lived down the road from us had a pet pig named Wilbur. The stark reality between pet and pork laid itself out in front of me at her house for dinner one evening when they announced we were having "Wilbur Burgers." I left in tears and arrived home winded and shaken. Mom tried her best to console me. The main course, which I had indignantly passed on, continued to haunt me. It took me years to erase Wilbur's memory, especially when an undeniable craving would come over me as the smell of fried bacon wafted from the kitchen.

County fairs were also a part of our landscape—the cotton candy, the midway lights, and the excitement of the annual outing for food, fun, and rides. This yearly event had it's own distinct smell and soundtrack. There was only one thing that could mar the joy of fair time for me and that was the livestock barn.

Hovering in each stall, young farmers in training faithfully and lovingly watched over and cared for the cows, pigs, and sheep they had raised from birth. Judging day would arrive. First, second, and third place ribbons were awarded for size and breed quality. And even before the ribbons could be put away, the prize-winning pets became pets no more. Loaded and crammed into trucks headed for market, slaughter awaited.

Give me the Ferris wheel and cotton candy on the sawdust-lined midway, but I avoided the livestock barns and all those big brown eyes that seemed to be looking directly at me for rescue.

Coming back to Indiana was bringing back so many memories and realizations. This morning's realization was that even into adulthood, I continued to be reticent about facing the reality of farm life and farm death.

163

Chapter Forty Two

"Ready or not, here I come!" was the chant we yelled as kids when we played hide-and-seek. It was a chant I still enjoyed remembering as an adult, and I could hear Father Christmas shouting it out now as the holiday season descended upon us. Dad busied himself lowering all the storm windows while Mom complained about facing another gray winter. But the cold was coming whether we were ready for it or not.

The Florida schools closed for holiday break and my girls were on an airplane heading to Grandma and Grandpa's house. The drive to the airport felt like old times. My parents and I had made it many times over the years. Dad wanted to go inside to meet the girls but decided he just wouldn't be able to walk that far, so he waited in the car as Mom and I found the little rascals just exiting the security area.

"Mommy! Grandma!" They squealed in unison. Both of them were dressed like matching dolls in their jeans and red sweaters, and we squeezed and kissed them as we took their hands and helped them with their backpacks.

"Where's Grandpa?" Chelsea asked.

"He's in the car, sweetie. He's not feeling real good today. But we'll see him as soon as we get your suitcase," I explained.

Bags retrieved, we found Grandpa outside opening the trunk of the car. As they spotted him and started running his way, their loud, happy voices could probably be heard throughout the terminal. I was afraid in their excitement they might knock him over, but he bent down on one knee as they approached and took them both into a bear hug at the same time. The scene touched me. I tried to hold back the tears, and I didn't dare look at Mom because I figured she was trying, too.

During our drive home, the car was filled with chatter and laughter. I was squeezed between my girls in the back seat. They couldn't get close enough to me. It was a competition to see who could get more of my attention.

Mom looked back from the front seat and asked, "Annie, did you ever tell the girls about the Christmas you surprised Grandpa and me?"

"Ooh, tell us, Mom. We want to hear the story," Chelsea begged.

"Well, it was during the time when I was a flight attendant. I didn't make plans to come see Grandma and Grandpa because I didn't have enough time off. At the last minute, I got an extra day free and decided I would surprise them on Christmas Eve. I called Uncle Jerry and told him about my plan. He picked me up at the airport."

"Did Uncle Jerry know it was a surprise?" Katie asked.

"Oh, yes. I swore him to secrecy. So when we got to Grandma and Grandpa's house, Jerry went inside and I slipped out of the back seat of his car where I had been hiding as we drove in. I ran into the garage, and just a few feet from the door to the kitchen I positioned myself. I stepped into a large green Christmas bag I had brought with me, pulled it all the way up and over my head, and held it there. In other words, I wrapped myself up as a Christmas present!"

The girls both laughed at this part. "Tell us the rest, Mommy!"

"Well, Uncle Jerry found a reason to have Mom and Dad go out to the garage, and when they opened the door, there was this big green thing sitting there. I let the bag drop to the floor as I yelled, 'Surprise!' Mom, do you remember that Dad scared the daylights out of me? He turned ghostly white. I thought he was going to have a heart attack!" I said.

"He didn't though, right?" asked Chelsea, her little face furrowed with concern.

"No, honey. Thank God, he didn't. I really surprised them, though. That was so much fun."

When we arrived home, the girls rushed inside to give Hooper some loving. Dad opened the trunk and I offered to help get the suitcases out because I had seen how he had struggled to get them in there.

"Thanks, honey. They are pretty heavy. You know your old pops can't lift what he used to."

"That's okay, Dad. That's what I'm here for," I said.

"You know you have two beautiful little girls there. They are so sweet. Regardless of how much you want to help your mom and me, your life is with those girls."

"I know, Dad. I know that."

But did I really know it? What if this was Dad's last Christmas? His last New Year's Eve? As a mother, my heart said, 'Go home.' But as a daughter, my heart was asking, 'How can you leave your mom and dad now?' I wondered how we would ever make it through this holiday. In my mind, I could hear my fellow recovery friends saying, "One day at a time. Just one day at a time. That's how we do it, Annie."

Chapter Forty Three

His granddaughters brought out an energy in Dad that none of us had seen in months. He tickled them, laughed with them, and gave them hugs and kisses. He walked them through the fields to look at the cows, the pigs, and the neighbor's horses. Hooper was always leading the way with her nose to the ground. Dad reminded her she wasn't a hunting hound, but she ignored him and pursued imaginary prey anyway. The girls delighted in trying to keep up with her, dodging dirt clods, mud, and deep crevices left by planting rows and farm machinery.

Anyone who knew Dad, knew he loved every kind of animal. In a part of the country where hunting was king, Dad couldn't kill a thing. He tried rabbit hunting, but couldn't shoot the little white-tailed creatures. He treated all animals with the care and respect most families reserved for their human counterparts. I wondered if this devotion stemmed from the fact that they couldn't talk back to him or because of their unconditional loyalty. Whatever the reason, his unadulterated love for them was hard to miss. No effort was too much, and no care was too great when it came to animals. Even the farm animals received tender-loving care. And the dogs were treated like kings. We'd had lots of dogs over the years, which I preferred over farm animals because there was no caging or slaughter involved.

Other families might actually purchase dogs, but the concept of buying a canine was foreign to us. We never found it necessary to buy one. Dogs came to us from every direction, in every size, shape, and age.

An injured skinny, yellow dog came limping out of the woods one day when I was in grade school. Dad said it looked like she'd been hit by a car. He could also tell she had recently had a litter because she was full of milk. Morning after morning he put out a bowl of food for her. The next morning it would be gone. After nearly a week of this routine, she finally started to trust him and even began to let him get close to her.

On the seventh day, Dad followed her into the woods, and sure enough he found them—four little pink, squealing puppies with their eyes still closed and eagerly awaiting the four-legged milk wagon that had led Dad to them. Dad bundled up the puppies, and along with Mother Dog, as we later named her, headed for home where the canine population had to be updated to eighteen. I learned the hard way that when it was animals versus kids, Dad always gave the benefit of the doubt to the animals.

Such was the case at a young age when I followed one of our dogs underneath a parked car. He evidently wasn't interested in my attention and he made his message loud and clear when he clamped down on the back of my head. With a bleeding head and a trip to the emergency room, Dad was quick to remind me that the poor dog was just trying to get away from me. The dog got his sympathy and understanding. I got fourteen stitches.

With the acquisition of so many dogs, there eventually followed a lot of doggie deaths. Blinded by my own grief, I didn't always see my father's pain. In later years, Mom would recount the dramatic effect the passing of each dog had had on my dad.

"Each time we lose a dog, your dad is devastated. It's really the only time I've ever seen him cry. I don't even remember tears at his own dad's funeral. But the loss of one of his animals brings him to his knees. I'm sure I don't have to tell the two of you. You've seen it. Your dad talks to his dogs and they understand him. I think he could teach them to do anything. He has a special bond with them," Mom said.

Mom waited until we were a little older before she told us the rest of the story about Dad and his companions.

Several towns from where we lived, an old deserted railroad track ran across the county, winding through mostly dormant cornfields and two-lane back country roads. Dad had a spot there where he could often be found when what today's doctors would call depression overtook him. Mom explained to us that these bouts of the blues were accelerated by his time spent with the bottle. If Dad was on a bender, which Mom called Dad's mini vacations where he drank for several days, she would drive to a spot where she knew she could find him. It was an overgrown area near the railroad tracks. Dad had buried several of his dogs there. Mom tried to explain to us that she thought this lonely spot became his sanctuary in times of reflection and sadness. He referred to it as a place to visit his pups. She described it as a place for him to wallow in the black hole of hopelessness that alcohol dropped him into.

Chelsea and Katie were taking turns brushing Hooper's coat when Dad asked, "Girls, I'm going to town for a newspaper. Want to ride with me?"

There was no hesitation as they yelled in unison, "Yes!"

"Can Hoop go with us?" Katie asked.

"Of course. She goes with me every time," Grandpa said. "She's my traveling partner."

I watched as they loaded into the pickup truck, a picture of happiness. I thought about how different he was with them than he had been with his own children. I was puzzled at when and what had caused him to change. It was such an improvement. My sister and I both agreed on that. Was it a natural result of maturity, or knowing he was ill? Perhaps he had learned from his mistakes with my sister and myself. We could only hope so.

Later that night, as I read literature from my recovery program, I ran across a description of acceptance.

And acceptance is the answer to *all* my problems today. When I am disturbed, it is because I find some person, place, thing or situation—some fact of my life—unacceptable to me, and I can find no serenity until I accept that person, place, thing or situation as being exactly the way it is supposed to be at this moment. Nothing, absolutely nothing happens in God's world by mistake...

When I finished reading, I tried to apply the principle to my relationship with Dad. If this premise were true, I realized for the first time that I played a part in the rift that had always been between us. It was a concept I had never considered before.

Chapter Forty Four

I read once that the dying aren't concentrating on dying—they're thinking about living every day. It's those around them that are concentrating on their dying.

Today seemed like one of the days where Dad was feeling good and concentrating on living life. He had recuperated from the grandchildren's Christmas visit and was busying himself doing normal things. He read the paper. He washed his truck. He paid bills. He was doing the living part as I struggled to not think about the dying part.

I was busy spending hours on the computer that I had brought home with me, researching Dad's particular cancer and possible treatments for it. I was becoming an info expert on a subject I had never longed to know anything about. Several times during the day, Dad sat down by me and asked questions about the contraption, as he called my laptop.

"This is called the mouse. It controls the cursor. See it move around on the screen?" I explained to him.

Dad's response was, "A mouse? That doesn't look like any mouse I've ever seen."

I showed him a couple of live camera shots of downtown Indianapolis. There was one live feed from an eagle's nest with eggs. Dad was fascinated with this one.

"That's unbelievable. What will they think of next?" he said.

It was fun watching him watch technology. I'd never seen many situations where he was rendered speechless, but this seemed to be one.

He yelled to Mom, "Hey Martha, did you know this damn computer has…what was that called, Annie? A mouse or a rat?" He laughed.

During Mom's earlier struggle with cancer, my sister and I were constantly looking for medical miracles on the Internet. We were spurred on by the fact that we came very close to getting Mom into a clinical trial. We contacted the resources, we did the paperwork, we did the follow-up. Meanwhile, when we mentioned the clinical trial to her doctor, he seemed to be unaware and uninterested that the program even existed. His lack of enthusiasm was frustrating, but I placated myself with the fact that doctors can't keep up with all the latest medical developments because they're busy making a living. This acknowledgment, however, didn't remove my resentment toward him. This was my mother's life we were talking about. It seemed reasonable to me that he should be aware of all the options. She should be his first priority. He should jump at the prospect of a clinical trial, just as we had. I asked myself what the hell was wrong with him? What about the Hippocratic oath thing? As it turned out, Mom was ineligible for the clinical trial because of another existing condition. We were disappointed, but at least we had tried an alternative, unlike the medical staff.

Now in Dad's case, we were being gouged with a two-pronged dilemma—the lungs and the liver, also known as cigarettes and booze. He hadn't had a cigarette in years, but apparently the damage had already been done. We searched the news and medical publications for any new treatments on these cancers. We scoured any source within our reach for alternate treatments and solutions.

One day on a morning talk show I heard an interview with an oncologist who was trying a new technique for liver tumors. I listened intently as he described the procedure of using radio waves to obliterate masses. He said they were having a lot of success with it. I grabbed a pen and paper and quickly jotted down his name just as

172

they went to a commercial. And then I just stood there too excited, too scared to move. It was the same feeling I'd had at age ten when I had a chance to win a shiny red bicycle. I knew the contest rules. You had to eat five saltine crackers and then whistle. The one that whistled first, won the bike. I gulped down the crackers, and then realized I couldn't take the next step because I didn't know how to whistle.

The same was true now. I had the doctor's name but I wasn't sure what to do with it.

Chapter Forty Five

Like the sound of a bell to one of Pavlov's dogs, the sound of Dennis's voice caused my heart to race. It was infatuation, yes, but also something more. After our first meeting at the pub, it was as if Dad and his illness, and all the details that went along with it, took a back burner on the stove. The front burners were occupied with phone calls and rendezvous with this new man.

Our first date rated a ten on my Richter scale. There was the beautiful, fancy restaurant; flirtatious and intellectual conversation; and of course that voice of his as dark and smooth as the chocolate on our decadent dessert that evening. I learned about his family, his education, and his law practice. He learned about my girls, Florida, and my ailing parents. We were soul mates from the salad forward.

"Mr. Dennis, you are quite a charmer, aren't you," I whispered across the table to him.

"Haven't met anyone like you in a long time." His words were measured and delivered without taking his eyes from mine as he reached across the table and took my hand into his.

Each night after I left him, the drive home gave me time to ponder and panic over the conundrum I was creating for myself. I chastised myself for what felt like a betrayal to my mom and dad. Time with Dennis meant time away from them. I felt dishonest and cheap. These same emotions had been the cornerstone of my alcoholic behavior. I asked myself, What am I doing? Where am I headed?'

In one of my frequent moments of insanity, I asked myself if I should go home and tell my parents about my new beau. I knew the answer was unequivocally no. I was sure my relationship with an African American would kill my dad quicker than any cancer could. So I always drove north to see Dennis. I never invited him to see me in Whiteland. In spite of my guilty feelings and leaving my purpose and folks behind, I was drawn to his company. Each time I began the drive to see him, the trip felt like a journey from darkness into light. I ignored the danger of the situation, but not the irony of it. I was leaving the white folks and heading toward the darker ones.

Since her office was close by, my sister would occasionally meet me in Indianapolis after work. There always seemed to be a game of cards going on at the pub, and she and I both loved to play. At least with that part of the story, I had been honest with my mom. It was either poker or a game called euchre, which is an Indiana favorite.

It must have been a sight to see my sister and me, the only two pale faces sitting at a table in the back surrounded by all black men hooting and hollering about the cards we'd been dealt. It was fun, but I knew it was also ridiculous. We were like children loitering on an unsafe playground. And on that playground, my sister met a gorgeous man who turned out to be a successful, well-known television news reporter. An African American news reporter. He invited her to a Pacers basketball game that was to be televised. She agreed, and we both sweated out the next twenty-four hours knowing that Dad never missed watching a game, and praying he and Mom wouldn't spot her on television with her date. The web we were weaving was indeed getting complicated.

The kinder families of our community called those with darker skins Negroes or black folks. They were referred to as living on the other side of the tracks. Their neighborhoods were called the dark parts of town.

My father was not always a part of the kinder community. The idea of whites and blacks mixing in any form or fashion wasn't right, and he wasn't too shy to tell you about his stand. His disregard and lack of trust and understanding for blacks reared itself up in foul language, racist jokes, and hatred. It was part of his core, just like so many his age. Basketball games were the only time he didn't verbally revile black people. He lived enough for basketball games to overlook the skin color of the players. But if they were on the opposing team, they bore the slang name that many of his generation used almost as frequently as the phrase "salt and pepper."

Dad loved to talk about the origin of town names in our community. Towns named Greenwood, Blackburg, Pinkerton, and Brownsburg all had a story. Our town was no exception. It started out as Wheatland and then became Whiteland. When it finally dawned on me that I had never seen a black student or black family within our city limits, I wondered if prejudice had been the catalyst for the name change. Perhaps Whiteland meant white folks only. That suspicion was confirmed when news spread that the Ku Klux Klan had left a flaming calling card in the front yard of a young black family that had just moved into town. I'd heard about the crosses they burned at unwanted families' homes but I'd never seen one. I also never had the chance to see their children at my school because they were forced to move before they even had time to enroll there.

"Birds of a feather flock together," Dad proclaimed. "You never see a chicken living or mating with another kind of bird. It wasn't meant to be that way. It's the same with people. Blacks with blacks. Whites with whites. End of story."

Chapter Forty Six

"Annie, the phone's for you," Mom yelled down the hallway where I was sitting cross-legged on the bedroom floor going through boxes of old photographs and school memorabilia.

"Thanks, Mom." I thought it was probably my girls. Since their visit, they had been calling every day asking how Grandpa was. Katie was particularly concerned about her Grampy and his strained relationship with his two older brothers. She couldn't understand why they hadn't been to see him since he'd gotten sick. We tried to explain the family histrionics, but it was a little beyond her comprehension. She just didn't buy it and wasn't letting go of the subject. I picked up the receiver and a deep, rich male voice said, "Hey, babe." It wasn't my girls after all. It was Dennis. Each time he called two emotions coursed through me—happiness, the lustful kind, and fear, the "what if they can tell he's black from his voice" kind of fear.

I reminded myself there was no reason for any debate or indecision on this issue. Our romantic entanglement could not be public. I was determined to go to any lengths to keep my parents from knowing I was involved with a black man.

"What do your mom and dad think about Dennis?" Joy asked me after we had been dating for several weeks.

"Huh! They don't think anything because they don't know anything about it. My dad is a mean son-of-a-gun. He would kill me if he knew."

When Joy didn't respond, I hoped I hadn't hurt her feelings with my comments. I'd forgotten she had shared her preference for black men with me. Her first husband was black, and her only child was a mulatto.

"My dad's not really mean. He's just old school, I guess. Everyone in his family is prejudiced," I said, hoping to cover my tracks. "We've always hidden things from my dad just to keep him from blowing his stack. Mom's a pro at it. Come to think of it, I probably learned my terrific deception skills from her."

I was relieved as Joy's cell phone rang, abruptly ending a conversation I wished had never begun.

We had a lot of taboos in our family and among them was the family phone bill. It was a well-known fact that Dad was not a great communicator, and communication for others was not one of his priorities, either. He disdained chitchat, especially if it had a dollar amount per minute attached to it.

Most of Mom's phone calls were just to my sister and me, but familial status garnered no hall pass from Dad. If he was the one to open the phone bill, the explosion that followed neared the magnitude fit for a global conflict or some other profound injustice. Mom defended herself by going to great lengths to prevent this scenario. She knew almost to the day of the month and the hour of the day when the phone bill would arrive. To our astonishment, her vigilance and precision in monitoring the postman's arrival often proved successful.

Like most of the mailboxes in rural areas ours was out by the road. No sooner had the mail lady stuffed her delivery into our mailbox and driven away, then Mom would hurry down the long driveway and snatch it. My sister and I were witness to her retrieval skills many times. Scurrying back into the house with her goods, we thought she looked like a mouse retreating into his hole after stealing cheese from a mousetrap.

"Mission accomplished," she whispered to us one day as she tucked the bill safely away in a dresser drawer. She had learned to reap satisfaction from the strangest achievements. I wondered if other mothers hid the phone bills, too.

I was wishing simple phone bills were my problem today instead of the insurmountable mission of keeping the existence of Dennis hidden far away. Our phone calls were sparse, short, and hush hush. I felt like I was leading two separate lives. There was a line of demarcation between my parents' world and the world where Dennis existed.

Long after I met him, I finally disclosed to my mom that I was seeing someone. I was careful not to divulge too much information.

"Are we ever going to meet this Dennis that you're dating?" Mom asked periodically.

Her inquiry made me squirm, even though I was expecting it and armed with excuses. Often when she asked me a question, I had the odd feeling she already knew the answer. This was one of those times.

I responded, "He never comes this far south. He's just too busy."

"Well, we'd like to meet him sometime," Mom said.

"Okay. I'll get him to come over some day."

As I left the room, I envisioned myself as a cartoon character with a thought bubble over my head. It read, "Come visit? Not in this lifetime! Ain't no way a black man is coming to a town named Whiteland."

Dennis had never asked to meet them and I certainly wasn't going to offer him up as a sacrifice. Dad was way too skilled at building bonfires to take that risk. So my sister and I continued to hang at the pub with the boys under the guise that we were just spending sister time together. It didn't feel right, but it was working.

Chapter Forty Seven

"You should leave early this morning, Annie. We got three inches of snow overnight and now it's sleeting, which will make the roads slick," Dad warned. He had his rubber boots and jacket on, and a funny hat with flaps that made him look like Elmer Fudd. The sight made me smile as he walked away.

My assignment for the church had ended and my new job had me reporting to an investment firm in downtown Indianapolis. The commute left me no choice about learning to drive in the snow again, and I forgot how cumbersome all the extra clothing and preparations are when you set out on a cold, windy winter day. I hadn't worried about losing winter gloves since I'd graduated from high school. Now here I was many years later looking for that one missing glove. It was similar to the search for socks that always disappeared from my laundry room in Florida.

Dad had a doctor appointment later in the day and Mom assured me they could handle it without me. I reminded her to take notes on what the doctor said. She said she would as she shooed me away with her hand.

"Get out of here or you're going to be late," mom chided.

My car windows were covered in ice and my hands were frozen by the time I cleared them. Where once a morning cup of coffee was simply a pleasure, I could see it was going to become a staple for survival. I stopped each day on my way to work and dispensed a cup of machine-generated cappuccino from the local gas station.

The taste wasn't epicurean quality, but the smell was inviting and my frozen fingers eagerly put a bear hug around the warm cup.

I found the building where my new job was located. As I greeted a few people on my way out of the parking garage, I could see my breath. I hadn't seen that in a long time. The frozen air coming from my lips reminded me of our pretend cigarette smoking days when we were kids. On the first cold day of the season, I could see us as we pretended to light up and exhale using our cold breath as cigarette smoke. It was fun, and we were all so used to seeing most adults smoke that it seemed natural. Some nights when Dad had a few beers under his belt and was in a lighthearted mood, he entertained my sister and me by blowing smoke rings from his cigarette. We loved it.

Julie and I also looked forward to trips to the grocery store with Mom where we could count on finding candy cigarettes in the checkout lanes right next to the chocolate bars. A little good behavior on our part might be rewarded with a box or two of cigs, as we called them.

At least in our household, cigarettes were used for medicinal purposes, too. The pain of an earache was treated with a blast of cigarette smoke into the ear. Mom explained it to us as we squirmed in pain. "My mom always did it when we were kids and it worked. I don't know why, but it does. Now hold still."

There didn't seem to be any talk that could persuade Mom otherwise. After all, she had also told us a story about the mysterious disappearance of her warts when she was young. She said that at least twenty warts had vanished overnight after they were rubbed with a new potato that was promptly thrown into a fire afterward. She pointed to the scars where the warts had once been. We found that kind of evidence comical, but indisputable. So my sister and I accepted the smoke treatment in theory and in our ears, but we didn't like the practice.

181

There was also another family tobacco story that we didn't talk about much. As a toddler, my sister had an unusual habit of eating cigarette ashes.

"Martha, you need to take that kid to the doctor. I've never seen anything like this. What the hell is wrong with her?" Dad asked in bewilderment. As usual, Mom followed Dad's orders.

The doctor was amused, but understanding at Mom's embarrassment. He explained that sometimes children and adults instinctively fulfill some deficiency in their diet. His advice? "Let her eat 'em." And that she did. She took her wet, pudgy little,finger and ran it all around Mom and Dad's huge ceramic ashtray, and then popped her finger into her mouth over and over again until there was nothing but cigarette butts left in the ashtray. As Dad shook his head in disapproval, Mom chirped, "Well, at least she doesn't eat the butts."

This morning Florida weather was sounding pretty good. Although I found few things more beautiful than waking to a snow-covered landscape, it was bitter cold and I wasn't looking forward to the rush hour traffic. As I left the house, large puffy flakes were still falling and creating a peaceful silence only a snowfall can bring.

The hub of downtown Indianapolis is called Monument Circle, a large circular plaza anchored in the center by a nearly 300-foot high limestone and bronze neoclassical structure built in the early 1880s in honor of Hoosier soldiers and sailors who were veterans of the American Revolution. Steps ascending to its base encircle the monument. On any given day, and regardless of inclement weather, the monument steps are filled with local folks reading, lunching, or just enjoying a respite from the workday.

Dennis and I had been seeing each other for a couple of months, and since his law office and my new workplace were close to the circle, we often met at a coffee shop there before work and sometimes at lunchtime. This morning I was feeling tired and defeated. No one had gotten much sleep during the night because Dad was restless and in pain. The smell of hot chocolate and flavored coffee wafting through the air was particularly comforting as I entered the shop and saw the recipient of my affection sitting over in the corner. He stood up and my heart sent a smile to my face. He was dressed all lawyerly—tie, black suit, and dark overcoat. He looked like not one, but four million bucks.

"Hey, babe."

"Good morning, handsome," I replied.

"How's my girl today? And how's your dad?" he asked.

Dennis always asked about my dad. Most days I didn't really know how to answer. It almost felt like a waiting game. Was he going to get better? Probably not. Did we have any options? Not really. I wasn't in the mood to talk this morning, so I closed my eyes and leaned into Dennis's warm embrace.

How must it feel to wake each morning and be met by the thought that your time is very short? It gave me a chill when I could bring myself to really think about it. I figured those were Dad's first thoughts each morning now. Instead of the warmth of the sunshine or perhaps the singing of birds that we are blessed with in the country, pain and death were surely foremost in his consciousness the minute he opened his eyes. The sicker he became, the angrier he became. My mom, sister, and I were growing increasingly sensitive to our conversations when we were around him. It didn't feel appropriate to laugh when he didn't have anything to be happy about.

But sometimes we forgot. After a funny story or watching my mom pull one of her capers, our laughter would fill the air. At these moments, the look Dad shot our way might as well have been an airborne knife. The weapon met its targets and the pain was keen. We scattered to another area of the house like guilty children banished to their rooms for misbehavior. No matter how hard I tried, I couldn't understand why he had to be so cruel. He treated us like we were his enemies.

Dennis's concern touched me. "Physically, he seems to be holding his own right now, but the depression is really starting to show," I said as he pulled me even closer to him. He hadn't lost either of his parents yet, but he seemed to grasp the overwhelming difficulty of the situation.

"Are the two of you getting along any better?" he asked.

"Yes and no. I don't know what to say to him and I think he probably feels the same way with me. When I think of something to talk about, I'm afraid of his reaction. He has a habit of belittling one's opinions. He has always had that effect, at least on me. He has a way of making you feel stupid and defensive. I can't seem to turn off those childhood tapes. As I say it out loud, I realize how ridiculous it sounds. It's stupid, isn't it?" I asked.

"Well, those tapes become a part of us when we hear them repeatedly, especially as children. That's why people have trouble at family gatherings. The adult children revert back to children because the sight of their parents and the familiar surroundings often trigger the old feelings and reactions. I've seen it happen in my own family. It's something a lot of us struggle with," Dennis said. "If we can convince ourselves that our parents did the best they could with the skills they were given by their parents, it makes the acceptance easier. Of course that theory is easy for me because my parents live so far away and I seldom see them," he said with a touch of humor and remorse, I thought.

"I did read an interesting article yesterday in the paper about a doctor in Miami. It caught my eye because a month ago I'd heard on television a story about this same doctor who is using a new treatment on liver cancer. Has something to do with using high frequency waves on the individual tumors. The article said he has been quite successful. So this morning I put a call into the hospital in Miami where he works asking them to have him call me."

"Wow. I hope they call you back," Dennis said.

"Me, too. I hesitated about even mentioning it to Dad because I'm afraid he will get his hopes up. But I ended up telling him anyway. We'll see. I'm keeping my fingers crossed."

"And how are your girls doing?" Dennis asked.

I stirred my coffee a little while trying to find the words to answer. "Honestly, I'm worried about them. Of course I don't get all the details over the phone, but they sound like they're running a little wild. Their dad works such long hours and travels all the time. I know he's trying to do a good job, but I think the reins on them are a little loose for their own good."

Dennis hadn't met my daughters yet, but I knew Katie would love him. Chelsea, I wasn't so sure about. The girls had seen me stumble through some pretty dysfunctional romantic relationships and marriages. There was the photographer who I relapsed back into alcoholism with, and a much younger man from Martinique who turned out to be a professional con artist. I suspected Chelsea thought any guy in my life was bad news. I reluctantly considered that maybe she was a little wiser than her mom in this area. I appeared to carelessly fall in and out of relationships. Sometimes I felt like a water faucet. Scalding hot with passion one minute, and then cold as ice the next like a faucet turned off and on.

"Our office is having a Christmas party. Will you come with me?" I asked him sheepishly.

"I'd love to, but are you sure that's a good idea?" he asked.

Puzzled, I asked, "What do you mean?"

"Annie, let's face it. Not everyone thinks the idea of you and me is okay. You know the old black and white thing."

"I know that, but you've already met everyone I work with. Please come with me," I whined.

"You're right. Hey, if you're okay with it, I am, too. What do we wear to this shindig?"

"It's cocktails at a colleague's house and then to a comedy club. How about your birthday suit? I'd like that! We could really give them something to talk about."

I put my arms around his waist and squeezed him as tight as I could. I had the desire to crawl right into his skin where I didn't have to think about anything other than him. I loved the way Dennis looked when he stopped by my office during the day. Often just coming from court, he exited the elevator and walked through the double-glass doors into our lobby. His height made him look statuesque in the same way Abraham Lincoln had looked, rather dignified and mysterious. He made my knees weak and my skin tingle like the feeling one gets in youth right before your first handholding or kiss.

The night of our first date had turned out to be a rather inaccurate preview of the real Dennis. Love him as I did now, I had no idea who he really was or how his brain worked. Being black in the 1950s couldn't have paved the way for an easy road to education. It appeared that against all odds, he had shown the drive and ambition to succeed at college and law school. And then after graduation it was as if his trajectory fizzled like a firework that is launched but never bursts into colors.

He practiced law with the discipline similar to that which I had for exercising—half assed, as my dad would say, and sporadic. His work as a public defender didn't seem to be motivated by challenge or any civic-minded passion. It seemed he settled for the position because it took less effort than securing private clients and provided just enough income to survive financially. Occasionally, I had the opportunity to compare his persona and lifestyle with that of other lawyers at the pub where we had met. He looked like the other attorneys, dark suit and briefcase in hand, but I suspected that's where the similarities ended.

I had no doubt he was intellectually brilliant. I clearly saw that quality and was attracted to and amazed by it. Like myself, Dennis had given up alcohol years earlier. He had the same story of most drinkers that find the need to quit. His life had become unmanageable. The difference between his sobriety and mine was that I was involved in a twelve step program and he was sustained by the "marijuana maintenance program."

"Hey, babe. I got a new case today. Gonna be defending a guy charged in a double homicide," Dennis explained. Killed a pregnant girl and her baby. What makes it even worse is that it was his girlfriend who was pregnant with his baby. There were two guys doing the shooting. My client and another guy. They're being tried simultaneously but with separate counsel."

I was intrigued with the details and the opportunity to watch him in court. My second thought was, would I want to be defended by someone who smokes pot all the time? Although he had never smoked in front of me, I knew he did it frequently. I figured part of his complacent nature came from its frequent use. Whatever the cause, Dennis's lack of drive drove me crazy. I saw such potential in him, but he didn't see it in himself. His car was older and in worse shape than the first one I had had in high school. He lived with a roommate (or girlfriend, I suspected), and often spent nights sleeping in his office on an inflatable mattress and bathing in the men's room one floor down in the building. He smoked incessantly and read voraciously. His former wife was an attorney as well and practicing in Boston, and he seldom mentioned his only son. I soon realized that he had little or no involvement in his life. I found his attitude toward fatherhood, and his lack of involvement in it, degrading and cavalier. He was a breathing, walking, specimen of an enigma, one I adored in spite of all the inadequacies and contradictions I perceived.

"You know your attitude toward parenting is the kind that helps perpetuate the belief that black men plant the seed and move on," I said to him one evening while we talked about his family.

He laughed and said, "You may be right, honey, but don't judge the whole race on my behavior. Besides, who appointed you as judge and jury?"

We both laughed but his comment gave me pause. Who was I to judge? Was that what I was doing with my parents as well? Judging them and then trying to change their lives?

I was still early for work so I followed Dennis to his office. As he lit another cigarette, I stood and looked out at the view from the window of his eighteenth floor office. The sun was setting and I could feel the cold evening air whistling through the cracks in the old window frame. For a fleeting second, I was caught in a time warp. My home was in Florida. I had two beautiful daughters that lived there as well. Where was I? How did I get here and what the hell was I doing? For a moment, just a moment, I forgot all about Dad and the cancer.

Chapter Forty Eight

We made it through the holidays. Christmas with children is always energizing and happy, and so was this one in spite of the grownups' misgivings. Each moment had a touch of bitter sweetness—gratitude to be spending time with Dad, and simultaneously fighting the thought that next year he probably wouldn't be with us.

Mom tapped on my bedroom door and said, "Wake up, sunshine."

"Morning, Mom."

"You've slept late this morning, honey. It's already nine o'clock."

"I didn't sleep very well last night. About two o'clock I found Dad in the kitchen rummaging around for Tylenol and saltines," I mumbled, still half asleep.

This wasn't unusual behavior for Dad. He was well known for his nighttime foraging in the kitchen. For years we had been laughing about his Twinkie story. One night, years earlier, when he hadn't quite finished his snack, he just took it back to bed with him. The next morning he staggered into the bathroom. Glancing up at the mirror as he brushed his teeth, he had quite a surprise staring back at him. Plastered to the side of his face was a half-eaten Twinkie.

"Your dad and his nocturnal snacks. God forbid we run out of saltines. He has a fit!" Mom said.

Mom and I were working on our first cup of coffee when Dad got up.

"Morning, Dad."

"Hi, monkey."

I noticed a grimace on his face and that he was holding his stomach. "Hey, I'm going to the farmers market later. Do you want me to get you some more pork rinds?"

"No thanks, hon. I haven't even finished the bag you got me last time. And my stomach is killing me," he said.

A short time later, I could see him out in the garage struggling to find something on his desk. I was reminded of many past days seeing him sitting there writing job proposals or talking to someone who needed electrical services. From an office with no power to a panicked farmer who was afraid he would lose his hogs if he didn't get the electric fans to work, he was always telling a customer he'd be right over. After the farmer's call, Dad explained to us that hogs, although pretty smart, will panic in extreme heat. He said they can actually suffocate when they are stressed by piling up on each other.

I was often confused when listening to Dad's phone conversations with his customers. He was friendly at first with the caller and most often had an answer for them no matter what day of the week or time of day. Then as he hung up the phone, he would swear like a sailor at the inconvenience, put on his work clothes, and head off to help them out. The local farmers, and all his customers, loved him because he was available, and *they* hadn't heard his aggravation like we had.

Mom and I grabbed our diet cokes and headed off to the market that was only a few miles away. Farmers markets in the Midwest are commonplace and a staple of life. On the way there, we passed several small wooden stands loaded with the vibrant colors of freshly picked fruit and vegetables. Farmers placed these stands in their front yards near the road in some cases, just yards from where they had been harvested. Stacked with fresh tomatoes, sweet corn, potatoes, and strawberries, I asked Mom to stop the car several times so I could take pictures of the beautiful colors. No need to inspect or squeeze these products like in the grocery stores. Here you could smell the freshness of the produce the minute you got out of your car.

"It's one of the things I think I miss the most about Indiana," I said to Mom. "We just don't have real tomatoes in Florida. Yuck. They have no taste."

In the fall, the same stands brimmed with pumpkins, gourds, and bittersweet. The honor system was always in effect with payment due, consisting of a straw basket or Mason jar where money was placed. Honesty here seemed alive and well because the routine hadn't changed in generations. That was another thing I missed about the Midwest. There was very little honor in south Florida.

Our destination this morning was a mixture of farm produce and flea market. Fresh green beans and radishes could be found right next to a stall containing old metal milk containers and an eclectic collection of antique buttons. Old farm tools, hand-stitched clothing, and stuffed animals from the 1960s were all waiting for you to take them home for just a few dollars. The smell of corn dogs, kettle corn, and cracklins or pork rinds, which is what we called pig fat that has been deep fried, permeated the air despite the fact that the market was right in the middle of an open field. The winding rows lined with vendors were delineated by a thick covering of sawdust. As I thought with excitement about all the treasures we might find, I also thought of where I might hide my purchases from Dad. Pork rinds and maybe homemade jam were all right, but any other items were met with disdain and verbal barbs.

Several weeks earlier Dad had suddenly started craving the cracklins, and since his appetite was waning, we were trying to accommodate any food request he had. We didn't know if the chemo and all the other medications had affected his appetite, or if a lack of will to live had dulled his desire to eat. I hoped we could find some treat he would enjoy.

The farmers market was packed this morning. The usual parking lots were full and blocked off, with excess vehicles parked up and down the sides of the road. Mom and I finally found a spot and started our hike to the entrance. I could smell the concession stands long before we got close enough to see them. With no baby stroller or dog on a leash, Mom and I were the exception to the crowd. We weaved our way up and down each carefully laid out aisle trying to take in everything on both sides of us.

"Mom, does Dad ever come to the farmers market with you anymore?" I asked as we rummaged through some old books.

"I'm afraid to ask him. You know how he talks. Rants and raves about someone else's trash and why would you spend your money on that, and then the next time I go he asks me to keep my eye out for something particular or to bring something home for him. I find it safer not to ask. It's a shame, though. I know he used to enjoy coming." She smiled as if a happy memory had just crossed her mind.

I stopped to admire some candles that looked like they were homemade. The female proprietor, a mother with two dirty toddlers hanging on to her, explained their fancy names and proceeded to give me her best sales pitch. The candles smelled worse than week-old garbage, but I didn't have the heart to say no. I bought two and found them a home in a dumpster near where we parked our car. I could hear Dad's voice saying, "Why would you spend your money on that?" But I knew Dad would have done the same thing if he'd seen that woman's face. He was a tough old bird, but he did have a heart—sometimes.

I recalled that many years ago we'd had a fight that started out over a mousetrap. I was between jobs in Florida again so I took the opportunity to visit my parents. Mom and Dad thought my boyfriend was watching my girls for me. What they didn't know was that he was actually my husband. We had secretly gotten married two years earlier. My new husband didn't care if anyone knew about the marriage, but I did because I was embarrassed to admit I was trying it again for the third time.

Mom and I were making the rounds of yard sales on a Saturday morning. It was always one of our favorite things to do on my visits. At the second house we stopped at, I spotted an oversized mousetrap. It literally looked big enough to catch a cat. Since we were having river rat problems where I lived in Florida, I bought it as a joke. Mom and I laughed all the way home about it, but when I showed it to Dad, he was not amused.

"What is wrong with you? Do you just have money to burn? Why do you buy that trash?" he spewed.

The conversation went downhill quickly. His nasty attitude knocked the wind right out of me. But this time, I didn't just slink away like the victim of a playground bully. I spewed back.

"Why do you have to say things like that?" I asked. "Why do you have to be so damned nasty?"

"Sometimes you act like you don't have enough sense to get yourself out of the rain," he replied from a face that had turned bright red. I realized his hands were shaking as he tried to close his desk drawer.

We yelled obscenities at each other and he slammed the back door so hard I thought it might break the glass. I walked to my room. When Mom came in a few minutes later, I was sitting on the bed crying.

"Oh, honey, don't you know better by now than to argue with that man? He's an ass," Mom said. "He took off in his truck. Probably headed for the bar. Should make for an interesting night."

Several hours later, after a few phone calls, Mom found out he and his brother had been drowning their sorrows in beer most of the afternoon. After she'd talked to Dad on the phone, she told me he was on his way home and was loaded and angry.

I panicked like someone trapped in a burning house. My breathing got shallow and I started to feel lightheaded. "I can't take it, Mom. I can't deal with him. I've gotta get out of here. He's going to be mean."

The odd part was, it would have been just as difficult for me if he had come home with an apology. All my life I frantically sought his love and validation, but I couldn't accept it if it was delivered in an alcohol-induced haze. That scenario felt like a bucket from the well coming up empty time after time. Ironically, I learned from Dad that sometimes you have to prime the pump at a well to get it started. His priming mechanism was alcohol. I desperately wanted his attention, but when it was tainted with booze, it repulsed me. Tonight I knew I had to get out of there before he came home looking for an argument. I began to pack up my belongings.

"But you're leaving tomorrow to go back to Florida, honey," Mom said.

"I know, but I can't face him tonight, Mom. I just can't. I'll spend the night at Julie's and she can take me to the airport in the morning. Call Julie for me, please, and tell her to come get me. Tell her to hurry."

With my suitcase by my side, I watched out the front door looking for Dad's headlights to come down the dark country road. I didn't have to wait long. Here he came. As soon as he pulled into the driveway on the side of the house, I gave Mom a hug and I slipped out the front door and hid behind some bushes near the road. Not long after, I saw my sister's car approaching. I stepped out of my hiding place and flagged her down. She never even had to come on the property. She stopped on the road and I threw myself and my bag into the back seat of her car.

Julie and I were both emotionally hungover the next morning as we headed to the airport. We cried and talked about the sad situation that was Mom's life. Once again, Mom was caught in the middle of the ugliness that was our family. She hadn't done anything, and yet we both knew she was the one who suffered when the miserable drunk came home. The sadness and anger on her face when I left the night before had not gone unnoticed. It killed me to hurt her, but I couldn't deliberately stand by and let him humiliate me again.

After that incident, Dad and I did not speak to each other for almost three months. It wasn't about the mousetrap. It was about all the other ugly words that followed during the exchange. If he answered the phone when I called, my words were, "May I speak to Mom, please." There was never any explanation given, nor apologies offered on either side. I never showed him anything I purchased from then on, except the pork rinds that were for him.

I added the mousetrap incident to my mental library under the title *The Bowels of Family Life*.

Chapter Forty Nine

M om and I were sitting at the kitchen table sorting through all of Dad's meds when my phone rang. It was Dennis so I excused myself and walked toward my bedroom.

"So how are things down there in the deep, dark south?" Dennis laughed as he asked. We hadn't had a chance to see each other during the day because he was busy in court.

"Well, we're plugging along here," I answered back with a nervous laugh as well. "Personally, I'm just trying to stay out of the crosshairs. Dad is grouchier than ever and I swear Mom is getting more contrary by the day."

"I wish I was there to give you a big hug. I can't imagine how hard this is."

"Thanks, Dennis. I appreciate it. Wish you were here, too. I'm so tired and confused. I could use a hug."

Later in the evening after dinner, I found Mom sitting outside at the picnic table holding her head in her hands. She was crying. I sat down with her, and when I asked what was wrong, she explained that her and Dad had exchanged angry words. She didn't need to describe the details. I'd heard the arguments many times before. Once again, he had used her as his whipping post.

"I was just trying to ask him about his next doctor appointment and he jumped down my throat. I don't care if he's sick or not, I can't stand him. He treats me like the enemy," Mom said as she dabbed at her eyes and then blew her nose. "There's just no reason for it. You know I should have left that man years ago. Do you remember I tried several times? Even filed for divorce once. Each time he would come crawling back a few days later begging for forgiveness and I would give in. What a sap I've been. I just didn't know how we would survive without him. I didn't have a job and didn't know if I could get one. I just felt trapped. Look where it got me."

I put my arm around her. "I'm so sorry, Mom. No one deserves to be treated like this. Try to remember he's sick."

But before I could finish she interrupted me. "Yes, but he's always been this way and he hasn't always been sick, at least not physically," she said through the tears that had started to flow again.

I told myself it wasn't a personal thing Dad had against us. He was angry at the whole world, with the difference being that the whole world didn't have to dodge his disapproval every day like we did. And his anger wasn't just toward Mom. The longer I stayed, the more the tension grew between Dad and me. This lead to more time spent with Dennis, which lead me to looking for more reasons to go back to Florida.

It didn't look like my presence was making any difference at all. His doctor appointments were less frequent now, and many times he didn't even want me to go with them. Mom would look over her shoulder at me and shrug as they walked to the car without me to leave for an appointment. Poor Mom, I thought. As she always had been, she was caught in the middle of a tug-of-war she hadn't started or wanted to be in.

I suspected Dad's insolence was not the only catalyst prompting my exit thoughts. During a phone conversation with my daughters, I discovered from one sibling ratting on the other that my four-teen-year-old, without her father's knowledge, took a taxicab to a downtown party on St. Patrick's Day. Katie explained to me that her sister was invited to meet friends and could only get there by cab. The two of them decided it was a risky and dangerous endeavor so

Katie armed her sister with a rolling pin, which they stuffed inside her purse just in case the cabbie was an axe murderer or kidnapper.

I didn't know whether to scream or laugh as she described the caper. But one thing I was sure of as I hung up, these girls needed more than a mother's voice on the phone. Their lives were running amuck, and looking back on my own personal experience, I knew it would only get worse.

After the call with them, I spent the next few hours drawing up a pro and con list, just like I had done several times before coming to Indiana. The list of pros for going home to my kids required an additional sheet of paper.

When I heard Mom and Dad come home, I tucked the paper deep into the bottom of my purse. I felt dishonest and sad. My brain felt like mush as I asked myself if I was coming or going. Was I running to or running away from something? Was I helping here or hurting? Was I here for Mom and Dad or because I was avoiding growing up?

In twelve step meetings people always talk about the committee in their head. I had a committee living up there and everyone in the group had a different piece of advice for me. I'd always felt lost and confused before, but never homeless like I felt now.

Chapter Fifty

My third and final job with the temp agency turned out to be an unexpected gem. I was to work as an assistant to the president pro tem of the Indiana state senate. Actually, it turned out all I was being hired for was to transcribe his dictation, but I felt like royalty, nonetheless.

During my other jobs in the city, I had ventured into the State Capital building several times. It was mammoth and regal. Every building back in south Florida was fairly new, but here they were old. I must have looked like an awestruck tourist as I climbed what looked like endless stairs to the entry and took in the massive marble columns and architecture of an era long passed. It was like a walk through history. I could feel the excitement. It was an incredible high. This was my first exposure to the workings of government and I couldn't get enough.

On days when the senate was in session, there was not a quiet moment. The senators and representatives scurrying about reminded me of anthills where the ants marched hurriedly here and there. These ants were sharply dressed in suits, carrying stacks of papers or briefcases, and each brow was etched deeply with a look of determination, or more often, a look of frustration.

It's hard to tell who's a farmer and who isn't when you put all the players in suits. But as I got to know them, I discovered most of the elderly men, who were called pages, were actually from my rural neck of the county. They were mostly blue-collar workers of retirement age and donating their time. Many of them had worked there long before I was even old enough to vote. Their responsibilities included answering questions, and greeting and guiding visitors to appropriate areas. There were one or two of them stationed near the chambers at all times. Sweet, unassuming, and polite, they were a breath of fresh air among the air of importance and ego that filled the hallways with elected politicians.

Before long, most of the pages knew my story of leaving Florida and coming back to help my parents. They showered me with words of sympathy and compassion.

"How is your dad doing, Annie?" asked Joe from his post at the senate chamber door.

These elder statesmen reminded me of the beautiful human spirit that is the Midwestern backbone. Many years spent in the south had made me forget that callousness is not standard operating procedure in all areas of the country. These sweet men wore their humility and kindness as naturally and consistently as residents in Florida wear sunglasses.

"He's holding his own, Joe. Thanks for asking. I told him you remember his older brothers. He got a kick out of that."

"It's a small world isn't it?" he said, and then turned to greet one of the arriving senators.

With a little bribing and a few flirtatious smiles, I worked my way into the chamber of the state supreme court to hear a case. I reminded myself to keep breathing as I timidly entered the chamber and took a seat in a chair old enough to surely have seated those in Civil War times. The air was heavy with mystery, judicial prestige, and formality. And although I was confused with most of the proceedings, the robes and the voices of authority echoing off the marble walls easily overrode my need for any comprehension of the case at hand.

I thought again of the gentle and strong human spirit that thrived in this part of the country. I was proud to be from a place with those wholesome values, but I found it almost impossible to reconcile this generosity with my dad's harsh tongue and rough edges. No doubt his father had imbued the same narrow-mindedness, acerbic manner, and prejudiced morals. After all I had witnessed many times and in many relatives, myself included, perpetuation of the Limp Attack, a name our moodiness and temper tantrums became known as. It was during my senate job assignment that the familial tentacles of racial prejudice found their way back to me. I'd felt them as a child, but had forgotten how ugly and pervasive they can be.

Enthralled and enthusiastic about the differences between where I had grown up and the metropolitan city I was now working in, I had convinced myself that interracial couples and upper-class blacks were being accepted without judgment. After all, the streets downtown were filled with blacks and whites working and socializing together. I noticed with great interest because it was a new sight to me.

However, I soon discovered prejudice was still lurking around every dark corner. It wasn't as bold and loud here as it was in other places I'd lived, but I could see it's ominous shadow in the office where I was working. Disappointment struck me as I struggled to understand the cruelty of comments I heard from some coworkers. Subtle racial slurs bounded about, and an air of superiority among nonblacks was obvious and tolerated without refutation.

As the shock of these observations began to wear off, I found myself questioning the possibility that I had always used my naiveté as a shield from things I didn't want to see or hear. I thought I had noticed stares as Dennis and I walked hand in hand around town, but my passion for him let any negative thoughts blow right past me like the cold winter wind that gave us a reason to walk a little closer to each other. I saw what I wanted to see and heard only what I wanted to hear. I was beginning to realize after many years of retrospection that I had always been driven by a search for some kind of refuge. Moving at careless speeds and with no itinerary, I missed a lot of life as I flew by it in search of the next resting place.

During my high school years, I was completely unaware of any of my classmates smoking, drinking, or engaging in sexual activity. Surely this was naiveté as it's best. Even though it was a rural school, I understood now that it was fairly safe to assume teenagers share the same hormones and attitudes regardless of the geographical area they live in. Somehow I missed all the abhorrent activities that must have been going on all around me.

During my airline years, I had been assigned a three-day trip working with a black male flight attendant. As innocent as it was, when we met for dinner on the first night of our trip, I felt like everyone in the restaurant was glaring at us. It didn't seem to bother him, but I found myself wishing we had worn our airline uniforms to show we were fellow crew members and nothing else. The second night of the trip, I resorted to being a slam-clicker as we in the airline called the unsocial crew members who slam their hotel room doors and click the locks shut, not to been seen again until the next day. I just couldn't handle another public outing with this dark man, despite the fact he was physically gorgeous, kind, and completely professional. My decision to avoid what I believed to be others people's prejudices felt safe, but not right. Now, many years later I was about to find myself in a similar position in the world of black and white.

Dennis and I met for a cup of coffee before work. Before we parted, we made lunch plans. It was Valentine's Day, and in spite of the cold weather, many people were dressed up in red hearts and offered holiday greetings in the restaurant and on the street. The date also meant the senate was about to adjourn their session and my job would be coming to an end.

Since Dennis had never met the people in my office, I asked him if he would come upstairs before we went to lunch so I could show him around.

He was quiet for a few seconds before he responded, "I'm not sure that's a good idea, hon."

"What do you mean?"

"Well, if you have any desire for one of the senators to offer you a permanent job, which you've mentioned to me, it might be best if I don't show up there," he said.

I suddenly realized where he was going with the conversation. "That's ridiculous. Several of the people in my office are black. It doesn't make any difference."

He raised his eyebrows and shook his head from side to side. "Honey, you're so naive. I've lived here a long time. Trust me. Maybe you don't see a black person when you look at me, but that's all they will see. The world's not as simple as you see it. You do not want me going up there with you."

I pleaded my case, but he was not to be swayed. Instead, we met up outside and sat on the steps leading to the Capitol building where he gave me a Valentine's card and a beautiful box of chocolates. His thoughtfulness touched my heart and made me happy, but his reluctance to enter what he obviously saw as a white world only made me sad. I was disappointed to realize that some people here in the city were just as judgmental as they were in my parents' area. I had idealized the acceptance of interracial couples because I wanted it to be that way. I wanted the world to be better than it was, just like I wanted my parents' life to be better than it was. I thought I had learned in recovery that one's acceptance is in direct proportion to their expectations. If that mantra was true, it was no wonder I felt irritable, restless, and discontent. My expectations were those of a fantasy world that existed only between my ears.

On my drive home from work that evening, a sense of aloneness came over me without warning and sent a chill through my whole body. I rolled up my car window, but the chill remained. It was a state of being that felt uncomfortably familiar. Not fitting in. Not having a purpose. Running away. Looking for refuge. I had successfully shelved those demons for a while by busying myself with my folks' needs. As those needs waned, I had become dependent on my relationship with Dennis.

Both of these facades were eroding away before my very eyes, and no matter how hard I tried not to acknowledge it, the erosion could not be denied. It was a lesson I had ignored over and over again in the past. It was like writing your name in the sand. No matter how many times you write it, the next wave always washes it away. This time was no different. In recovery circles, it's called insanity—doing the same thing over and over and expecting different results.

Once again, I was lost between the world of being a child or becoming an adult. It made me stop and wonder which person my parents saw me as. Instead of caring for them, was it possible they felt like they were babysitting me?

Chapter Fifty One

S ince the day I'd mentioned to Mom and Dad about contacting the Miami doctor regarding a new treatment possibility, a palpable sense of anticipation and fear had moved into our house. We strongly avoided the subject while knowing it was the one thing we all wanted to talk about it.

It was 3:52 p.m. on a Friday.

My memory is much less than stellar. I don't easily recall birthdates or appointment times. But on this day, the details burned themselves into my mind. My cell phone rang. I recognized the 305 area code. It was a Miami phone number.

As I answered, I walked to my bedroom and closed the door. To my surprise, it was not an assistant, but the Miami doctor himself on the other end of the line. I tried to keep my voice calm as he explained how he had gone over Dad's medical records and his history. He said there was a very slim chance his procedure could help. " In your dad's case," he explained, "I'm afraid the outcome is not what you're hoping for."

His words sucked the air right out of my lungs. I leaned toward the bed and braced myself against the wooden footboard. With my finger, I began to trace the outline of the music and Jesus stickers that had been there since I was a teenager.

He couldn't help us. He was sorry, but if it were his father, he explained, he wouldn't put him through the procedure. There were just too many tumors. I thought, How many are too many? I thanked him for his time and his call, and said good-bye. Paralyzed, I continued to hold the phone to my ear long after there was no voice on the other end.

I don't know how long I cried, but it was long enough that it had gotten dark outside and Mom was calling me for dinner. She probably thought I had laid down for a nap after I disappeared with the phone. Panic set in. What should I say to them? I hated myself for ever calling that doctor. I hated the doctor because he didn't have the answers we wanted. I hated cancer.

I dragged myself into the kitchen and joined my parents at the red and white plastic tablecloth that had been around for as long as I could remember. Dinner included cubed steak, corn on the cob, cottage cheese, and Dad's favorite—mashed potatoes. Right before "Would you like some iced tea?" and just after "Please pass the butter," I delivered the news from the doctor.

Mom and Dad said nothing. They didn't need to. Their faces wore the words that couldn't be voiced. We sat there in silence through the remainder of the meal trying not to look at each other. Our hopes had crumbled and the potatoes had turned cold.

Chapter Fifty Two

The longer we dealt with Dad's illness, the more time and space lost its clarity for me. Yesterday felt like months ago, and tomorrow seemed years away. The big world seemed small, and our small town seemed huge and unfamiliar. The days melted into nights. Weekdays overlapped weekends. Fear morphed into grief and then turned into more fear.

Life was beginning to feel a little like an amusement park where there was no one manning the on and off switch on the rides. There were days that reminded me of the Tilt-A-Whirl. At first, the spinning was fun, but eventually it led to nausea and even throwing up as I had done once as a child on that very ride. Today everyone in the family was spinning on the Tilt-A-Whirl because no one was at the controls, and in this case, the ride was cancer.

Then there was the Ferris wheel. Dad loved to take us on this ride when we were little. All cars must inevitably stop at the very top as they load on new passengers at the bottom. My sister and I knew what was coming but it didn't make it any less frightening for us. Poised motionless at the top, which seemed like a hundred stories above the ground, Dad would start to rock our seat back and forth. We held on with a death grip that made our fingers numb as we begged him to stop. It happened every year, and every year he managed to talk us into doing it again. Insanity had us in its grip then, just like it did now.

We were so proud of Dad in his younger years when he shot hoops at the fair trying to win us a stuffed animal. When he won, he was as proud as a peacock, and when he lost, he walked away cursing about how the whole game was rigged. Mom said we knew Dad's routine as well as he did. She also commented one year that it's sad when the cotton candy doesn't taste as good as it used to, but that was part of growing up. I didn't understand those words at the time, but now looking face to face at mortality, I got it. Cancer was forcing us all to grow up. We were trapped in the chaos of the fair's midway and freak shows, and we just couldn't find our way out of the park. The amusement rides were no longer amusing, the disease was no longer arrested, and our anger was no longer passive. P. T. Barnum once said, "Every crowd has a silver lining." I couldn't see any silver in this crowd. Perhaps then, we were all colorblind.

I was getting ready to leave for work one morning when Dad yelled from the bedroom, "Annie, wait. I want to ask you something."

He held out a sheet of yellow paper from a legal pad and I tried not to notice how much his hands were shaking. He had drawn brackets for his picks for the NCAA basketball tournament. His handwriting was easily recognizable. He always printed his letters. "Do you have access to a copy machine at work?" he asked.

"Sure," I said.

"Do you think you could make a couple of copies of this for me?"

I took the paper from him and said, "Of course, I can. These are the teams you think will win?"

He smiled and said, "Yep."

This was a good sign. Even illness couldn't squelch Dad's love of basketball. I overheard him on the phone several times discussing with his buddies and his bookie some of the college games that were coming up. Even when I couldn't see his face, I could hear the passion in his voice as he talked about which colleges had been paired up for the opening rounds. March Madness, as it's called among basketball fanatics, had arrived with all its excitement and histrionics.

That evening as I struggled to go to sleep, I kept thinking about Dad's basketball charts. Basketball games had four playing periods called quarters. Was it really possible we were we looking at Dad's last quarter, or would there be an overtime? When I finally went to sleep, I dreamed about a game. But the game was football, not basketball, and more importantly, there were no overtimes and no winners.

Chapter Fifty Three

"Chelsea, please let your sister have a turn," I scolded into the phone. I could hear Katie crying in the background because Chelsea wouldn't hand the phone to her.

"Mom, I'm not done talking to you yet. It's still my turn. Katie, shut up! I can't hear what Mom is saying!"

By the time Katie finally got her turn, she was sobbing and all I could do was try to console her. Chelsea had always bullied her, but it seemed to be getting worse the longer I was away from them.

"Mommy, I miss you. Chelsea is mean to me and Dad always takes her side," Katie cried. "I know you need to help Grandma and Grandpa but I want you here. Could I come there and live with you?"

The pain in her voice cut through me. I could imagine her little face all wet and splotchy from the tears. I wanted to hop on an airplane and be there in an instant to hold her and dry her tears. I could hear Chelsea in the background still mouthing off and I asked Katie to put her father on the phone.

He confirmed my suspicions. They were increasingly tormenting each other and acting out in other ways. It was the first time their dad had ever asked me when I was planning on coming home. For a proud man who lived squarely on the basis of self-reliance, I had to smile when I recognized he was silently yelling "UNCLE!"

I'd just gotten off the phone with my girls when I looked over at Dad at his usual post in the corner of the sofa. The leather sofa, which had once been a rich butterscotch color, was now a pale yellow from sun and age. It had a matching footstool that was always covered in newspapers. It didn't look like Dad had gotten to any of them, though, because they were all still folded in their original state. It could have been my imagination working overtime, but I thought he looked unusually pale and his movements were listless.

It was Sunday afternoon. As usual the television was on but the volume was down all the way. I never figured out why our family sat around looking at a television screen with no sound, but we often did.

We heard a knock at the front door, a sound that always startled us because no one who knew us ever used our front door. As kids we called it the preacher door, and the formal living room next to it was the preacher room. This was as far into the house as any traveling religious zealots would get when they came calling. Neighbors and friends, even the UPS man and the mail person, knew to use the back door that led into the garage. Packages were left on top of the dryer.

But this day, Mom, Julie, and I had a pretty good idea of who was knocking at the door. We knew because we had made the appointment, and although we had discussed the decision with Dad, no specifics were mentioned so he had no idea that today was the day. We answered the door and our first meeting with the hospice representative began.

Flashing through my mind was this scene that looked like a bad movie I'd squirmed through once with all of us sitting around the living room—Mom, Dad, and my sister on the sofa, and me seated in a rocking chair that my Grandma Nellie had used when she was alive. Our visitor sat in Dad's green recliner. It seemed like only yesterday that Dad would come home in the middle of the work day to have a sandwich and then a quick nap in that recliner. He had apparently passed on to me the art of being an on-the-spot napper. Give Dad or me fifteen minutes and we could take a fourteen-minute nap.

I was afraid to look in his direction as I said, "Dad, this is the person from hospice we mentioned to you. She's just here to give us some information."

She shook our hands and introduced herself as Virginia, the patient advocate from Hospice Care of Johnson County. She looked like one of the church ladies that were a part of my grandma's congregation. She wore a light blue suit with a nametag on her left lapel identifying her as a registered nurse.

The reality stunned me. I could barely catch my breath and my mind froze like the face of a clock when the electricity goes out. The voices around me sounded like one of my old 45 records that would get stuck on a scratch and keep playing the same music over and over. Had I been asked, I probably wouldn't have been able to even state the day of the week, but I knew without a doubt that I would never forget the light blue shade of this woman's suit or the piercing green color of her eyes as she gazed at one of us to the other.

When I finally made myself look Dad's way, he was still and expressionless. Dad's countenance reminded me of one autumn when Mom and I took advantage of my free airline passes and visited Madame Tussaud's Wax Museum in New York City. Now looking at my dad, I would not have been able to discern the difference between his face and one of those wax figures we had marveled over. Tussaud's models were of celebrities we'd never met. But this wax figure had the eerie likeness of my dad.

Nurse Virginia talked. We listened. She left some paperwork for us.

The house was quiet after she left. We went our separate ways with no discussion. It was as if she had never been there.

My dad's decline was undeniable. It was only thirty days later when hospice knocked on our door again, but this time the visit was decidedly different. There was no community gathering in the living room. The nurse was here to see a patient, a very sick one.

After tending to my dad, the nurse emerged from his room and spoke to us in a quiet voice, obviously trying her best to be specific but gentle as she described the signs we might begin to see in my father as his condition worsened. She explained the changes would be small, but markers of his decline.

"What is your father's favorite thing to drink?" asked the nurse.

Nine months ago the answer would have unequivocally been beer. Today our answer in unison was iced tea.

"Near the end he will probably stop asking for tea. He will only want water, and even that request will come less and less often," she explained to us. "He will start to sleep more often and longer. His desire for conversation will start to wane and small things will aggravate him."

Of course she had no way of knowing that big and small things had always aggravated him. She continued to speak softly and slowly as she explained that it was probable we would start to notice Dad staring off into space or looking down at the floor for long periods of time.

"Why is that?" I asked, finally mustering up the courage to use my voice.

"We're not sure why, but it seems to be a common marker as the cancer progresses. Don't let this discourage you from talking to him. He will still hear you and sometimes answer, but don't be surprised if he doesn't respond. It may be tempting for you to withdraw as he does, but try not to. Your love and your touch will be comforting to him even when he doesn't acknowledge it."

I was trying to hang onto the nurse's words, to try to remember what she was saying, but my head was spinning and making me dizzy. What was she saying? He would quit drinking tea? How the hell could she know that? How could she know he would start looking down at the floor? Was it possible all cancer patients have the same reactions?

I felt a great sense of respect for this woman and her courage to do this work. I sure couldn't do it. But I couldn't help but question the validity of identical behaviors in the terminally ill. Terminally ill. What a horrible phrase. I could only picture the word in huge, ugly black letters. With the human body so advanced and complex, how could anyone possibly know dying would bring about these specific behavior changes?

Then I remembered pediatrician visits when my children were young. At each specific age—two months, ten months, fourteen months—the doctor pointed to a chart on the wall that listed the behaviors each child should be exhibiting for that stage. At four months—smiling. At ten months—disturbed sleep patterns. At fourteen months—separation anxiety. It was amazing how accurate the markers were.

What month was Dad in? Ten months from the end? Four months? I wanted to ask the nurse how long Dad had, but I knew if I spoke, the nausea would exit my body in an unsightly manner. I tried to bring myself to admit that I had already noticed his waning interest for his beloved newspapers. And as incredulous as it appeared to all of us, his attachment to Hooper was diminishing as well, despite the fact she refused to leave her master's side.

Chapter Fifty Four

Aside from the rumor mill of a small town that flawlessly operates twenty-four hours a day, people were starting to notice Dad's absence. I could hear Mom fielding phone calls daily, where in hushed tones she described Dad's condition to his concerned friends, relatives, and customers. She was doing her best to remain cordial with everyone, but with each call, I could hear the wear and tear in her patience.

After a particularly long conversation where Mom had been forced to keep repeating herself to the person on the other end, my sister Julie leaned over and whispered to me as she pointed toward Mom who was just hanging up the phone, "She's ready to blow!" And blow she did.

"I can't take any more of these calls, kids. They're driving me nuts," she said as she fumbled in her purse for her cigs. "The same people asking the same questions over and over. I bet your Dad didn't answer my relatives' phone calls or questions when I was sick." Her face was flushed as she looked over at my sister and me. "Well, did he?" she gruffly asked.

"Uh, I can't remember, Mom. Let me answer the phone for you. I'll talk to them," I said, trying to disguise the dread in my voice.

"Hey, Mom, has anyone found mushrooms yet?" my sister asked in an obvious attempt to change the subject.

"Not that I know of. Uncle Jerry has gone hunting a few times, but hasn't found any in his usual spots. It may be too early. Sure would like to have a nice mess of them, though. Even though he isn't eating much else, I bet your dad would eat a few mushrooms," Mom said. "I felt so sorry for your dad. Jerry came by one day last week to ask him if he wanted to go with him to hunt mushrooms, and your dad just shook his head no. I do believe that's the first time in all these years I've ever seen him turn down a trip for mushrooms. I cried after Jerry left. Of course I didn't let your dad see I was crying. He would have made fun of me," Mom said as if tears bringing ridicule was standard procedure.

The mention of mushroom season brought about the fondest memories for me. My family waited for mushroom season with the reverence and anticipation others saved for hunting season. These weren't the same mushrooms you could find in the grocery store. They were wild and rare mushrooms. Every spring, dedicated mushroom hunters pulled over to the side on country roads, found themselves a good sturdy stick to poke through the brush with, and traipsed in and out of wooded areas looking for the treasures that were often buried under wet leaves or fallen tree limbs. Your find was called a mess, and the bigger the mess you brought home, the better.

I loved mushroom hunting with Dad. It was one of the times when I felt closest to him. He was relaxed because he was in his favorite space, outside, and because he was relaxed, he was patient and kind. It was a real adventure.

Each year on our first mushroom hunting trip, Dad would explain to me once again that the secret was to find the first mushroom. He promised that after I found the first one, it would be pretty easy to spot them. Sounded like a plan, but I didn't find it that simple. The more mushrooms he spotted, the more monotonous the ground looked to me. Eventually, seeing my frustration, he would point me in the direction where he had already seen a few and let me find them.

"Someone's already been over this area," Dad would say, pointing with his stick at some underbrush that appeared to have been tamped down by human feet. "But that doesn't mean we won't find any here. These suckers grow so fast that yesterday they might not have been here, and today they'll pop right up, especially after a good rain."

I found the smell of the woods to be intoxicating. I thought maybe Dad found it that way, too. It was a mixture of the sweet scent of new spring growth and the dampness left behind by the winter's snow. But the fact didn't escape me that the same elements that produced this smell attracted snakes and spiders. I knew the sticks we carried weren't just for poking about in the undergrowth. They were to let the snakes know we were coming. Dad explained it was better to let a snake know you're there than to scare him or wake him up. Better to have him run or bite the stick rather than your leg.

"Hey, you guys, do you remember the snakes in our yard after the floods?" I asked Mom and Julie. My sister's answer reminded me that she was too young to remember much of the childhood I remembered, so I filled her in with the gory details.

Each time after Sugar Creek flooded, snakes were left behind on our property. As soon as our yard dried out enough to be cut, Dad would crank up the lawn mower and invariably run over a snake or two. Many times my sister and I spotted snake body parts flying into the air. At first startled himself, Dad always seemed to recover quickly just in time to enjoy our squeals of horror as we ran back to the house. He would never admit to a fear of the slimy creatures but said he had respect for them. Respect or fear. In this case I didn't see any difference between the two.

"Okay, enough of the snake stories. Girls, do you want a soda?" Mom asked Julie and me as she poured herself a glass.

"Sure, Mom. Thanks. Did I hear someone come in while I was in the shower?"

"Yes. It was Tom Brewer. Do you remember him? He used to work for your dad years ago. I just don't know what to tell people when they call or stop by. Sometimes, if Dad's awake, he doesn't mind company. But most of the time, he complains after they leave, and I can understand why because it wears him out. I shudder each time I hear someone at the back door. I know people mean well, but sometimes they're just stupid. They come too often and they stay too long, just like your Aunt always used to do. If your Dad were his old self, he would say of those kind of visitors, 'They don't have the common sense to get themselves out of the rain, and they don't know when to leave.'"

We all laughed as we recounted the times we had gotten phone calls saying Auntie was on her way for a visit. We all bickered over who had to stay and babysit her, and who was the lucky one that got to leave before she arrived.

"I think we even drew straws a couple of times," Julie said, and laughed.

"Oh, we're so bad!" Mom said as she glared at both of us with mock disapproval.

"How about we make a note explaining that Dad isn't up to visitors and then you can tape it on the back door when you need to when he's not feeling good or you guys are napping. What do you think of that idea?" Julie asked.

"Well, we can try it. I think most people will just ignore it and come in anyway," Mom mumbled as she lit another cigarette. We had all given up on trying to convince her to quit smoking. She said she didn't want to quit and that was it.

"Well, the note thing is worth a try," I said. "Let me find some paper and we'll make the note right now."

As I worked on printing the message, I found myself thinking that once Dad was gone, there wouldn't be anyone knocking on the back door anymore. What the hell were we going to do with Mom when Dad was gone? We had been so preoccupied with his diagnosis and treatment that we hadn't had much time to think about the future. How would Mom survive without him? He was a monster sometimes, but he was her monster, the one she leaned on for everything.

I finished writing the note. It read, "We appreciate you coming by but Garold is not feeling well enough today to have visitors. Thank you. We love you. Martha and Garold." Staring down at the note, a silent panic spread through my body like the feeling of Novocain as it slowly numbs your gums, then your tongue, and right on down to your throat. This was real. We had decisions to make. Big decisions. We couldn't put the reality off much longer.

I looked out the windows of the garage. They were dirty. Dad had always kept them clean. Even through the dirty windows, the world looked so pretty outside—green and lush. And although my eyes were registering the beauty of the sight, it couldn't erase my brain's image of the journey through a dark tunnel we found ourselves taking.

Chapter Fifty Five

The silence that descends upon the landscape during the winter season started slowly disappearing with the hum of spring activity. It was a strange juxtaposition for us. Spring, normally the farming community's time for hope and a new season of crops, found us struggling to welcome its beginning as we simultaneously edged toward the end of Dad's life.

There were many days when I found myself wondering how the rest of life could be carrying on so normally. It felt insulting, and made me lonely to think that while we were experiencing our own hell, the rest of the world was doing what they had always done. Kids caught the school bus, mothers did the grocery shopping, and police monitored their beats while we watched Dad getting sicker every day.

Local farmers began cranking up their tractors and combines. Motorists began bemoaning the onset of crowded two lane country roads where slow-moving farm machinery made it nearly impossible to pass and often created a parade of impatient cars. But no one honked their car horn. It was an unwritten rule that during this time of year farmers owned the roads. And, respectfully, farmers would often pull to the side of the road when they were able to, allowing cars to pass them safely. It was not unusual to hear locals bragging to outsiders that this was another example of Midwestern courtesy.

On their spring break from school, Chelsea and Katie arrived to spend the week with us. Before they arrived, I found myself asking and wondering if this might be the last time they saw their grandpa.

Dad's deterioration was accelerating on a daily basis now. He was exhibiting less and less energy, more detachment, and just like the hospice nurse had warned, fewer requests for food and his beloved iced tea. We couldn't tell if the changes were of a purely physical nature or the advance of depression and resignation. Either way, Mom, Julie, and I took turns crying and hovering together in fear and gut-wrenching sadness that permeated our every breath.

Chelsea and Katie arrived and we tried to take solace in their visit. Even Grandpa's illness could not squelch their bright spirits and energy. Although, in quiet moments, I could see their thoughts were heavy when they sat next to him on the couch, hugged him, and held his hand. I couldn't imagine the depth of their understanding of the situation. Dad still responded to them much more so than he was doing with the rest of us. He smiled when they talked and tried his best to embrace them before he eventually would explain, "Honey, Grandpa's tired. I'm going to take a little nap."

The girls' visit proved to be a timely one for Hooper because Dad's attention toward her was waning as well. The more distant he became, the less Hooper sat at his feet. Dad had instilled in me that dogs have a keen intelligence and intuition, and Hooper's actions were proving his theory. She seemed to sense she was losing him, that the two of them had made an agreement that it was time to let go. She left her spot at his feet to follow the girls' every move. At night when she had always slept on the bed with her master, she slipped into bed with the girls where she was met with absolute delight.

During their visit, I realized once again how complicated and sophisticated the minds of children can be. Children, and animals, always know and understand much more than we give them credit for.

Overhearing our conversations, Katie had become aware that Grandpa was not on good terms with his older brother Otto. A cocktail of brotherly riffs and alcohol had been a constant deterrent to family peace for many years. Although she had never met this uncle, and without our knowledge or help, she set out to find him and make things right.

"Mom, you know Grandpa's brother Otto..."

"Yes, honey. What about him?"

"I looked his phone number up and I called him," she said.

"You did what?" I asked in shock.

"I called and told him I was Garold's granddaughter, and that I wanted him to know that his brother was very sick and that it would mean a lot to Grandpa if he came to visit him."

I saw the tears well up in my sister's eyes as she stood up from the table and put her arms around Katie.

"Honey, what a sweet thing to do. That had to take a lot of courage. What did Otto say?" Julie asked.

"He thanked me for calling. He asked me how old I was and said I sounded very grown up. He said he hoped he could meet me one day. He said he was very sorry that Grandpa was sick and promised he would come to visit him. Do you think he will?" she asked.

"I don't know, baby, but at least you tried. I'm so impressed you did this on your own. You're something. Did Chelsea know you were doing it?"

"Yep. She said not to because I was going to get in trouble, but I did it anyway," Katie said, looking very pleased with herself. "Why don't Grandpa and Otto talk?"

My sister replied, "Oh, families are complicated, honey. Little problems get blown out of proportion over the years and then stubbornness and pride cause adults to act like spoiled children. Sometimes we treat those we love the most in a way we wouldn't even treat strangers. It's sad. Thank you again for what you did, honey. We can all learn a lesson from you."

Later in the evening, when everyone had gone to bed, Julie and I hashed over our earlier conversation with Katie.

"I still can't believe Katie called him. You know who I was really referring to when I said we could all learn a lesson from Katie's phone call, don't you?" Julie asked.

"I suppose you mean the old goat," I responded. I realized we hadn't called Dad by his nickname since he'd been sick.

"Yep. I pray to God that I don't treat my own family like Dad has treated us all these years. It's not a legacy I want to carry on. I know it's a mean thing to say when he's sick, but it's true. Do you think he has ever realized how he's treated us? I mean, is it possible he didn't see how angry and cruel he was so much of the time?"

"I don't know, Julie. The truth is we will probably never know. I'm sure he learned it from his dad. Look how he and his brothers have treated each other. I also know it doesn't make the hurt any less. I don't think Dad ever wanted to be mean. I think it was out of his control somehow." I could feel a knot forming in my throat. "In recovery there's a lot of talk about breaking the cycle. They're talking about the cycles of abuse, addiction, and family dynamics that endure generation after generation. They get it from their parents, they pass it on to us, we pass it right on to our kids, and so on."

"Damn, that's a scary thought, but it makes sense. Sometimes I hear myself and I sound just like Dad—impatient and sarcastic. I don't want to be like that. I don't want my kids to walk around with the scars you and I have. Let's face it. You and I are screwed up!" she said as she laughed.

I joined in her laughter and then said, "I wanted so much to share some of my recovery with Dad. Last year when I came home and made my amends with him, I planned what I was going to say. Then when I sat down with him, I froze. I think the old childhood tapes started to play and fear of rejection or criticism paralyzed me. Just like now, there are so many things I'd like to ask him, so

223

many things I'd like to say while we still have a chance, but I can't get the words out of my mouth. I let him put a damper on every conversation. I always have."

"Do you think Otto will really come to see Dad?" Julie asked skeptically.

"I don't know. I would if I were him. I can't think of anything worse than having someone die before you can make peace with him or her. Do you know what I mean?"

"I do. That Katie sure loves her grandpa, doesn't she?"

"That she does. I hope he knows that. I hope he knows how much all of us love him despite the battles we've had," I said.

Julie said, "He knows, sister. He's tough on the outside but there's a heart in there somewhere."

I went to sleep that night thinking about my sister's words and, ironically, the movie the *Wizard of Oz*. It had always been one of my favorites. I thought of the Tin Man. He had an oil can that looked just like the one my dad had. He and my dad had several things in common—the oil can, and sometimes the no heart thing.

Chapter Fifty Six

The evening before the girls were returning to Fort Lauderdale, we were enjoying a perfect spring evening where the air was crisp and the sunlight was soft and warm. Hooper scurried around the yard chasing newly arrived bugs and butterflies while the girls packed up their belongings, intermittently arguing about who got the window seat on tomorrow's flight.

Mom and I could still see the neighboring farmer on his tractor where he had been working all day in the field behind our house. We had started to go inside when we both noticed the sound of the tractor getting closer. As we turned to look, we saw he had driven right up to our property line and was now walking toward us. We were about to discover that neighborly kindness had arrived to lend a hand.

"Hi, Mrs. Limp. I heard Garold is sick. I'm finished with that field and was wondering if you'd like for me to till his garden for him?" asked the man in dusty overalls and a flannel shirt.

"Oh, my God. That would be wonderful, even though I don't know if we'll get to use it. Thank you so much. I'm going to go wake him up and let him know," Mom said as she headed back toward the house.

I watched as it took the farmer only a few minutes to turn the soil following the footprint of Dad's previous gardens. When he finished, he turned and waved, leaving through a neighboring field.

I sat down in the grass with Hooper and cried. It wasn't crying at the movies kind. It was the kind that erupts from your toes and comes out like the sound of a wounded animal, unbridled and inconsolable. Hooper sat close and licked my face. She never licked, but this time she did. She recognized the pain. It was a combination of neighborly kindness and helplessness that brought sadness to the surface. The garden was Dad's thing. It always had been. It was his territory. It was his love. It was his pride and joy. But it never would be again.

I'd lost track of how long I sat there in the grass when I realized it had been some time since Mom had gone into the house to get Dad. I started walking back to the house just as my sister's car and my uncle's truck pulled into the driveway right behind each other. I heard the sliding glass door open and saw Mom and Dad making their way outside. Mom was pointing to the garden. Dad was shaking his head from side to side in disbelief. I spotted a tear slowly making its way through the stubble on his pale cheek.

For his sake, we all forced our sadness to give way to celebration. It was time to plant a garden.

"Dad, where do you keep your seeds?" I asked.

Before he could answer, Chelsea and Katie were asking, "Can we plant the seeds? Grandpa, can we help do the garden with you?"

"There's packets of seeds in the barn," Dad said, "but do you guys really want to do this?"

There was no question, at least in my mind. And the girls agreed as they both ran to the barn yelling, "We'll find the seeds!"

Uncle Jerry helped Dad take a seat behind the barn in an old nylon lawn chair a few feet from the garden's edge. His precious seed packets were brought to him and placed in his lap. It occurred to me that from a distance the scene probably looked like a king surrounded by his court.

Still in the wooden drawer where they were stored all winter, each seed packet was precisely marked in pencil with the name of the plant and the date of purchase. There were lettuce seeds, corn seeds, and watermelon seeds. The tomato seeds were marked with specific names like beefsteak and Brandywine. As an adult, just like as a child, I knew nothing about the difference between tomato varieties except that they were red, yellow, or green. But every year since I could remember, Dad was religious about educating himself with the plethora of seed catalogues that arrived early every spring. Some of his seeds were years old, but Dad said it didn't matter as long as they were stored in a dry, dark place.

For a few moments that afternoon, we all got to forget about the cancer. Dad took charge. With the alertness and energy we had watched previously wane, he began picking which seeds to plant and giving instructions on how deep and far apart in the soil was appropriate. Even though he was giving the orders from his chair, he sounded a little like the old authoritative Dad I realized I actually missed. His granddaughters were enthusiastic about their new role as gardeners. A few times Dad gently chided them when he saw the rows they were planting were not straight.

"Hey, girls. Watch how you're planting those rows. They have to be straight. Uncle Jerry, help them straighten out those rows of lettuce, will ya?"

Katie looked up to yell, "Okay, Grandpa. We'll make them straight. Can we come back to help you pick the vegetables when they're ripe?"

"I'm counting on it, honey. I'll need your help because your ol' grandma sure can't do it!"

"Excuse me, I know how to garden. I've picked many tomatoes in my time, so there," declared Martha in her most commanding voice. We all laughed at the thought of her in the garden. It was as likely as seeing her in the cockpit of a jetliner.

The sun was just starting to go behind the tops of Dad's tall pine trees as the last seeds went into the ground. We all took a moment to look at the masterpiece, including Chelsea and Katie who were covered in dirt from head to toe.

I understood why Dad had such a passion for gardening. The smell of the rich, black soil and the promise of green sprouts appearing any day were Mother Nature's magic show. The other magic we had just witnessed was still sitting in the old lawn chair, exhausted, but looking happy and proud. I offered to help Dad walk back to the house and, for once, he didn't refuse the help. As soon as he stood up, it was apparent he would need more than just me to make it back. The afternoon had worn him out. With his older brother Jerry on one side and me on the other, we slowly half guided and half carried him away from his garden. Although I tried to ignore negative thoughts, they wouldn't be denied. I was pretty sure he would never make it back to that square patch of dirt that he had always thought of as his little piece of heaven.

As I tucked the girls into bed that night, Katie asked me, "How long does it take for the plants to grow?"

"In a few days we should start to see them pop out of the ground," I whispered to her as I stroked her forehead.

"But we won't be here when all the plants get big."

I sat down on the bed next to her. "You can come back. Close your eyes now, baby. Time to go to sleep."

"Mommy? Will Grandpa be here when the tomatoes get ripe?"

I closed my eyes and buried my face in her sweet-smelling hair. She was waiting for an answer and I couldn't find the strength to give one.

"We'll talk about it tomorrow, honey. Remember the song I used to sing to you?" I asked.

"I do," she whispered back.

"Close your eyes, honey. I'll sing it until you go to sleep."

Chapter Fifty Seven

From the moment I'd arrived at my parents' place, I was amazed and amused at how many items in the house had never been moved, even an inch, over the years. Mom never denied that housekeeping wasn't her thing, and the dust piled on shelves and books undeniably backed up her claim. Every house usually has at least one junk drawer, but all of Mom's drawers had this designation. The linen closet, the pantry, and her bedroom closet all looked as if they'd had an explosion inside. When teased about it, she would say, "Tidy is not my forte!"

I'd learned one important lesson during my career du jour in real estate—unlike the house I'd grown up in, the importance of a clutter-free property was a priority. If you wanted a quick sale, you needed to insist on no messy closets, few if any knickknacks on the counters, and no pets or any sign of their existence. Also prohibited were refrigerator doors cluttered with photographs, children's artwork, and magnets of any kind.

As I glanced over at Mom and Dad's refrigerator, I knew we were lucky that their house was not on the market because their refrigerator door was covered in magnets of every shape and size. Many of them were yellowed, and I suspected they had resided there for some thirty or forty years back to when I was still in high school.

But today there was only one magnet of any importance on that refrigerator. It was a small, unimpressive Farm Bureau Insurance magnet. Held underneath it was a small scrap of white paper with columns for names, days, and time. It was a list of shifts for what might be called Dad's babysitters. It was a list I never dreamed I would live to see. It was confirmation of our family's crossing over the threshold from cheering squad to caretaking battalion.

We all trusted that Dad wouldn't see the list on the refrigerator because he wasn't making it to the kitchen very often now. His routine was basically from the bed to the bathroom, and occasionally out to the living room. It was still a shock each time I saw him trying to get himself out of bed. He no longer had the walk of a man with a purpose. He shuffled. His skin and face had become colorless and gaunt. I wanted so desperately to reach out and help him when I saw how weak he was, but he still had his pride and I knew better than to try to cross that boundary.

I remembered the morning when I'd seen Dad emerge from the bedroom dressed in his first pair of Levi's and tennis shoes. Spurred on by his younger brother's dip into the fashion world, he proudly strutted out showing off his new duds. Laughter replaced my tears as I thought about how the name of tennis shoes and Levi's had evolved since that morning many moons ago. Since the shoes weren't just for tennis and there were many brands of jeans, the old names had become as antiquated as the three hundred pound, fifteen-inch thick television sitting in my parents' living room. Everything changes, and yet nothing changes. I couldn't decide which annoyed me more.

In recovery, I'd learned that hatred and defiance toward change are common and dangerous characteristics among alcoholics. I likened the situation to being thrown out of one's lifeboat without the ability to swim. Change meant the risk of resentment and lack of trust, both of which had played a role in my drinking career. Feeling out of my comfort zone had always been eased by that first cocktail. Dad's condition had all of us way out of our comfort zone.

I checked the schedule on the refrigerator. Mom's shift watching over Dad was each morning from 7 a.m. to 10 a.m.; Julie's shift was

10 a.m. to 3 p.m.; and my shift started after that. Every other day my cousin Vicki would be our relief pitcher.

It was on Mom's first night watch that Dad woke up in such pain that we had to rush him to the emergency room. Mom drove while I tried to reassure him.

"Where does it hurt, Dad?' I asked.

"Annie, I can't even tell. I hurt all over," he said.

I could see how scared he was, scared enough to have tears welling up.

After an examination and a shot of pain medication, he was released to go home. Mom and I gave each other a knowing look. The medical staff didn't verbalize it, but we knew. There was no treatment left for him. All that could be done was to make him comfortable. We had just seen palliative care in action.

The pain meds started to kick in as we prepared to leave and Dad commented on how comfortable the hospital bed was. The next day, I ordered a hospital-type bed from hospice, which they promptly delivered that afternoon. The hospice worker had not even made it out of our driveway before we got a taste of Dad's disapproval. His anger was directed at me for what he viewed as my impulsive action in getting the bed.

"Why in the world did you get this?" he asked with obvious disdain. "Once again, your mouth was in gear before your head was."

It was as if a beast had arisen from out of that frail man. And even though I'd heard his cruel words many times before, they tore through my heart. Paralyzed, I stood in the middle of the living room staring at him. Surprise, shame, and embarrassment stupefied me and the old voices in my head started their badgering. The voices shouted to me, "You're stupid. You're worthless."

I ran from the room without saying a word. Maybe the restraint of pen and tongue part of my recovery program was finally starting to kick in. I was the target but I hadn't fired back. I knew of no weapon or language to describe or defend myself from that kind of pain and verbal terrorism. So, like I had seen Mom do so many times over the years, I escaped, seeking refuge far from the hospital bed and the eruption of the spewing volcano.

Although I tried to avoid him, our paths crossed several times that evening. I could tell he regretted his earlier words to me. He went out of his way to make conversation, asking if I wanted to read the paper and if I had talked to my girls. I wanted so much to believe he was trying to say he was sorry, but he either couldn't or wouldn't say the words. His pride ran deep. I understood that part of his personality because, unfortunately, it was part of my personality, too. Our pride and stubbornness were the evil twins, and a steep ravine ran between us. It was a ravine so deep that even now, so close to the end, we weren't able to cross.

Chapter Fifty Eight

If a dog can be sullen, Hooper was that. Since the day the hospital bed arrived, she refused to enter Dad's room. I didn't blame her. The truth was that I was trying not to go in there, either. The sight of the small, lifeless form lying on crumpled sheets in a stainless steel bed wasn't like a walk through the park. "Dogs aren't stupid." I could hear Dad's words once again.

I was grateful that I had a few more weeks of work ahead of me if for no other reason than to get out of the house. Dad's doctor appointments had become less frequent, and it seemed without those outings he was quickly slipping further into another world where, try as we might, we could not reach him. In the Midwest, people talk about passing the time by watching paint dry and corn grow. It felt like Mom and I were participating in those exciting activities. We were spending more and more time just sitting around looking at each other and watching television.

I was delighted when Dennis phoned to tell me he had a homicide trial scheduled to begin in the next few weeks. It was something to look forward to. His client and another young man were charged with shooting and killing a pregnant woman in a drug deal gone sour. The details were grim, but I had to admit that I was looking forward to seeing him in court. Regardless of how much I tried to conjure up the image of him as an attorney, I couldn't picture it. I didn't tell him why, but I knew. For some reason I couldn't make a dark-skinned Perry Mason come alive in my imagination.

My sister and I discussed the possibility that Dad might read Dennis's name or see his photograph in the newspaper. Dad hadn't asked too many questions about the man I was spending a lot of time with, but he did know his name. And my sister was walking on a similar tightrope because she was still seeing the black local newscaster.

"We are so bad! Dad would kill us if he knew we were both seeing black men," Julie said with a grimace.

"No joke. I think Mom suspects because of Dennis's voice on the phone. It's so deep, but she's got so much on her mind that I think she forgets about it right after she hears it. She has finally stopped asking me questions about him for which I'm grateful."

My sister's and my actions were so incongruent with the circumstances around us, it must have looked like we were leading double lives. We both admitted it was uncomfortable feeling exhilaration and guilt at the same time in regard to our social lives.

"The truth is I've always gone in the opposite direction Dad wanted me to. I think at least half the decisions I've made in my life were based on rubbing him the wrong way. Isn't that an awful thing to admit?" Julie said as she used her hand to make a gagging motion toward her mouth.

A sigh was the only response I could come up with. Maybe the flirtation with danger was blunting our pain. Maybe the excitement of our unacceptable behavior was helping us to avoid an involuntary look at mortality.

The week before Dennis's trial began, I asked him to join me at a twelve step meeting where I had been asked to share my story of recovery. I was pleasantly surprised when he agreed without hesitation. Although he had given up alcohol years before, I didn't believe he had ever been to one of these meetings. He sat in the front row as I shared my story of drunkenness and recovery. Afterward, when we got in the car to leave, he reached over and gently laid his hand on my leg.

"I want to tell you something. I just want you to know I have never been more proud of anyone in my life than I was of you tonight. Hearing you speak, telling your story, made me realize how very important your sobriety is. I hope you know that I would never do anything to jeopardize that. I heard tonight how you've worked so hard to get where you are. I've never loved you more than I do right now."

His words were so sincere. I thought I saw a tear in his eye. For a moment, any burdens in my world vanished as I melted into the comfort and safety of his adoration.

We were quiet on the rest of the drive home, but there was a silent conversation going on between us. The words didn't need to be spoken. We both knew, at least in our heads if not our hearts, that our relationship was coming to a fork in the road. My job was ending. My dad's life was ending. My time in Indiana was ending. And our relationship, well, it was probably ending, too. Ah, the tangled webs we weave, I thought.

Although there had been brief conversations about my living in Indiana or his moving to Florida, we both knew it would never happen. We were emotionally attached by only a frail thread. Our passion was fierce, but not enough to thwart the knowledge that our paths were too divergent to ever cross indefinitely. We both recognized there would be too much collateral damage on my side to ever make a permanent move. We were rooted in our respective lives and locations.

To keep my heart from beating right out of my chest, I pulled myself closer to him and silently recited the Serenity Prayer over and over again for the rest of the drive home. "God grant me the serenity to accept the things I cannot change, the courage to change the things I can, and the wisdom to know the difference."

Chapter Fifty Nine

Despite the fact that I was excited about my daughters upcoming visit, it took me awhile to recover from Dad's stinging words about the hospital bed. The night of the incident I woke up having a panic attack. I realized the shock of it all had acted as an unexpected catalyst, moving me in the direction of my next step.

I got out the pros and cons list I had started the previous month. I had an important item to add to the con side. I'd suddenly realized that if I didn't go back home before Dad passed, my departure would be at the height of Mom's grief and I wasn't sure I would be able to leave under those circumstances. My sister agreed.

"Sis, you've really done all you can here. God knows I'm not looking forward to it, but I can handle things with Mom when Dad is gone. You and I can talk on the phone when there are decisions to be made. You need to get back to your girls. You know Dad feels the same way. Think about it. Talk to Katie and Chelsea about it while they're here. It will be easier to leave before Mom loses Dad. We both know that."

"I'll think about it, Julie. I'd better get going. I'm happy the girls are getting to come visit again and their flight lands in an hour," I said looking down at my watch. It felt like the world was moving at such a fast pace. There were moments when I didn't feel like I could keep up with the speed.

On the way to the airport Dennis called. The jury in his trial was back and he was headed to the courthouse to hear the verdict read.

"Call me as soon as you hear something."

I heard frustration and a nervous edge in his voice as he answered, "I will, hon. Say hi to your girls for me."

While waiting on the girls' flight to land, and as we left the airport, I continued trying to call Dennis but got no answer. We were hoping he would have lunch with us, so we decided to just drive to his office and surprise him.

When we arrived and knocked several times on his office door, there was no response. But since we could hear voices inside, I opened the door just a crack and peered in. A wave of smoke billowed out and engulfed my daughters and myself. It seemed we had caught Dennis easing the pain of losing his case with an afternoon session of his marijuana maintenance plan. One of the boys was found innocent and one was on his way to prison. I had to wonder if the other attorney had won the case because he was drug free and clear headed.

I quickly pulled the door shut and hurried my girls back to the car, all the while trying to explain to them why we had left so abruptly. My mind was whirling and my knees felt weak. Although I was pretty sure the girls hadn't understood what was going on, I was so embarrassed. Thankfully, the girls quickly forgot about what they had just seen and talked incessantly all the way home. I joined them in the chatter, but I really didn't hear a word. Nausea welled up in me each time the image of Dennis's shocked face flashed in front of me. I was disappointed for him and myself. Once again, my heart had not synced with my head. How could I have gone down this path? I wanted to run and hide.

After dinner Chelsea came outside to the picnic table and sat with me.

"Mom, are you mad at Dennis? Is that why you were so quiet all afternoon?"

"I'm not mad at him, honey. I feel sorry for him and that makes me sad."

"Okay. I love you, Mom," she said as she took off toward the house.

"I love you, too, honey. Come back here and give me a big hug."

Later in the evening, I finally answered Dennis's phone call. Our conversation was brief and on the surface, emotionless.

"I'm sorry about what happened this afternoon. The attorney defending the other kid won his case and I lost mine. I wasn't coping very well. I hope your girls weren't upset. I felt like such a fool. I so wish that whole scene hadn't happened. Look, I told you before, I recognize how hard you've worked for your sobriety. I would never forgive myself if I messed that up for you. You're not saying much. Are you still there, Annie?"

"Yes, I'm still here. I don't know what to say. I'm just listening."

"I love you, Annie, but we both know we have no place to go with this. I think we've known that since the day we met. Be with your Dad, love your girls, and then go back to Florida. That's what you have to do. It's where you belong. I'll keep you and your family in my prayers. Take care of yourself, hon. Bye."

I heard the dial tone and he was gone. That was it. The love affair that had begun so unexpectedly, and probably inappropriately, had ended just as abruptly. It felt like a great movie with a bad ending. I was numb. I knew sadness, shock, and anger were only moments away, but as I hung up the phone, I locked away all those emotions behind some door that I had no key for.

For the next three weeks, I watched my dad deteriorate, and I watched my own mental state do the same. It was alarming to see how dependent I had become on Dennis, and how much I had been burying my sorrow about Dad by focusing on my obsession with him.

A frenzied, desperate sense of aloneness drove me to countless failed attempts to reach out to Dennis. I called him incessantly. I drove by his office morning, noon, and night. It was old behavior. It was behavior indicative of my drinking days. Guilt overwhelmed me. I was here for my parents and all my energy was being directed toward this man who had, in no uncertain terms, already said good-bye. In a few rare moments of sanity, I knew Dennis had made the wise decision for both of us, but the pain of losing him kept me flailing with wild imaginings of different endings to our story.

I wanted to escape. I wanted to run away from everything that hurt. To run to anything that lessened the pain. I thought of alcohol, but turning to alcohol was not an option this time. My heart was aching and my head was grateful for my recovery program. I remembered the words I'd heard in recovery, "Pain is the touchstone of growth."

Finally, in the silence of reflection, a gift of sobriety, and being able to be present in the moment, I was able to let go of thoughts of Dennis. At long last, the reason I had come back to Indiana became foremost in my mind once again. I thought maybe my task was completed here. Maybe it was time to go back to my life. Mom and Dad had trudged along on their journey for years without me there to guide them. Maybe it was time to let go of them, too.

Just as I had when I decided to rescue my parents nine months earlier, I made a pro and con list. Ironically, it contained almost identical items in each column. This time what had been a con was now a pro, and vice versa. I needed to return to my daughters. I would be starting over when I got there. Looking for a job. Looking for a home. Looking for a new beginning. I wanted someone to tell me that I was making the right decision. I wanted to know that my choice was not based on the broken relationship with Dennis. I wanted to make sure I wasn't running again. I needed to know that I wasn't giving up on my purpose for coming here just because I was in a bad mood or that my thinking was clouded with depression. It was a frightening realization that these were questions I had never had the ability to ask myself before. I didn't have the answers, but at least I had the clarity to ask them.

I sat down with my parents and explained that it might be time for me to go home. We talked about my pro and con list. They did not need to be convinced. We were all on the same page. It was time for me to leave. Mom cried and Dad simply sighed.

The following day I began to pack a few of my belongings that I would take with me on the drive back to Florida. And as sick and weak as he was, Dad insisted on going over a checklist with me about the condition of my car. Oil. Water. Tires. We concluded that the car was in good shape. I concluded that I was the one that needed repair.

The day I left will be etched in my memory forever. I was as uncertain of my actions as I was the day nine months before when I'd left to come here. But I did sense this time that things would be different when I returned to my children and my life, because I was different. I had used the excuse I was coming back to help my parents because they were sick. But finally, I was able to recognize the truth. That truth was that I had come running back home as a child seeking refuge. It was an intuitive response borne of fear, abandonment, and the ties that bind us in hopes of redecorating the past.

I believed this time, for the first time, I would be leaving my parents as an adult. Maybe, after facing up to old childhood scars, I would be bringing with me a little more acceptance and forgiveness of my parents and myself.

We said our good-byes at the back door. I will never forget how frail Dad felt when I hugged him. There was still so much more I wanted to say. So much I needed to say. But the only communication available now was the shedding of tears.

I had been on the road less than an hour when my phone rang.

"Hey, honey. How are you doing?" Mom asked.

"So far, so good, Mom."

"Your Dad had something he wanted to tell you. I'll put him on."

"Hey, Annie. In case I didn't say it, I wanted you to know that we really appreciated you coming home and spending this time with us. I know it wasn't always smooth sailing, but I wouldn't have had it any other way. Give those grandbabies a hug for us. Drive carefully. I love you, Annie. Always have. Always will. Remember that."

Chapter Sixty

Dad didn't make it to the beginning of summer. Just as his corn grew tall and his beloved tomatoes began to ripen, we said good-bye to him.

His memorial service passed in a blur. On a cloth-covered table in the front of the room where his friends and family had gathered, we placed his tool belt, a pack of chewing tobacco, and a picture of Hooper. They were a few of his treasured possessions.

The room was packed. I recognized many relatives, but there were so many other faces I'd never seen before, many more friends than I even knew Dad had. Their words to Mom, and Julie, and me were simple and heartfelt.

"Your dad meant so much to us."

"We sure will miss him. He helped us out so many times."

"You know your dad was one of a kind."

"He played hard and he worked hard just like the rest of the Limp boys. He was a good man."

As we gathered ourselves to leave, I turned to look back at the now empty room one more time. Just as the lights dimmed, I could have sworn I heard Dad's voice whispering, "This is the end of the story, Annie."

Chapter Sixty One

Sometime after Dad left us, I received a letter from a cousin who had lost his own father at a young age. He looked up to my dad and loved him like a father figure. In the letter he wrote:

"I just wanted you and Julie to know your dad talked about you all the time. I'm sure he didn't say it often, if at all, but he was very proud of both of you. Remember that."

My cousin's simple words were like salve to an open wound. That's all we'd ever wanted to know. That he loved and appreciated us.

In the long days that followed, I made a conscious decision not to remember the mean dad, or the one in pain, or the one in the hospital bed, or the man so frail and weak.

I chose to think of him on our trip to Las Vegas where he flirted with the skimpily clad waitresses unabashedly and stared in awe at the number of high-rise hotels. I pictured him in San Francisco where he, Mom, and I had taken a ride on the streetcars and laughed as we passed the steep hills and crooked streets. I saw him staring out at the ocean in Florida where we teased him about his skinny white legs, and how on every trip he mentioned at least once that he couldn't believe the beauty and vast wealth of the area.

I saw his rough hands with their cuts and scars from a life of manual labor—a truck polished to perfection, and trees trimmed with precision and care. I saw him bent down embracing one of his many dogs, and showing with his actions an unspoken respect for all of God's innocent creatures.

Chapter Sixty Two

With the passage of time and the completion of this manuscript, many of my wounds have healed, and some memories have become blurry and hence less painful. As I suspected, I returned to my daughters with new insight about being a parent, and a renewed fervor for my program of recovery that had enabled me to survive during such an impossible time.

It seemed Dad's departure had not turned out to be the end of the story after all, although I'm sure Dad might have found it necessary to disagree! Amid my own struggles, I saw him in me, and myself in him. There it was—the moodiness and discontentment, and the inability to control either. We both had the same symptoms. He was never diagnosed with a treatable mental disorder, but now, many years later, I had been.

After my diagnosis of depression and rapidly cycling mood swings, I knew in my heart that Dad and I had both suffered from the same demons. Dad was forced to carry the mental burden with him to the very end. I was fortuate enough to get professional help to allow me to heal. Finally, I had found the missing piece of the puzzle to the man I called my father, but not until I found the missing piece in me.

It was not the end. It was the beginning of a new chapter. It was a time to plant a new garden like Dad looked forward to every spring. It was a chance for renewal where grace and appreciation could mature, and understanding and forgiveness could triumph over the pain and errors of humanness.

"This is the grace of the last years—the children coming to understand the contradictions in their parents, not to reconcile them but to encompass them in a larger love."

Janet Sternburg

About the Author

L ee Ann Ropes grew up in Indiana but has spent most of her adult life in Florida, where she works for a major US airline. While impatiently awaiting grandchildren from one of her beautiful adult daughters, she continues to write and photograph.

www.limp73.blogspot.com www.Laropesphotography.smugmug.com

CPSIA information can be obtained
at www.ICGtesting.com
Printed in the USA
FFHW020807300419
52157038-57526FF